A Place in the Lodge:
Dr. Rob Morris, Freemasonry and the Order of the Eastern Star

A Place in the Lodge

*Dr. Rob Morris, Freemasonry
and the Order of the Eastern Star*

UPDATED EDITION

Nancy Stearns Theiss, PhD

Westphalia Press
An Imprint of the Policy Studies Organization
Washington, DC
2018

A Place in the Lodge

A Place in the Lodge for me;
A home with the free and the bright;
Where jarring cords agree,
And the darkest soul is light:
Not here, not here is bliss;
There's turmoil and there's gloom;
My heart it yearns for peace-
Say, Brothers, say, is there room?

My feet are weary worn,
And my eyes are dim with tears;
This world is all forlorn,
A wilderness of fears;
But there's one green spot below,
There's a resting place, a home,
My heart it yearns to know,
Say Brothers, say, is there room?

I hear an orphan's cry,
And I see the widow's tear;
I weep when mortals die,
And none but God is near;
From sorrow and despair,
I seek the Masons' home,
My heart it yearns to share,
Say, Brothers, is there room?

With God's own eye above,
With Brother-hands below,
With friendship and with love,
My pilgrimage I'll go;
And when in death's embrace,
My summons it shall come,
Within your heart's best place,
O Brothers, oh give me room

A place in the Lodge for me,
A home with the free and bright,
Where jarring cords agree,
And the darkest soul is light.

Dedication

To my best friend and outstanding father, grandfather, and husband Jim Theiss who patiently helped me edit this manuscript.

To Marjorie Morgan Applegate, a real mover and shaker in the Order of the Eastern Star who has spent her life making the world a better place.

CONTENTS

Acknowledgments ix

Introduction xi

Chapter 1: Brother John and Sister Charlotte 1

Chapter 2: Love and Marriage 17

Chapter 3: Life in the Antebellum South 29

Chapter 4: A Pivotal Time for the Morris Family 51

Chapter 5: A Masonic Career 69

Chapter 6: The Conservators 91

Chapter 7: The Order of the Eastern Star 107

Chapter 8: Rob and John 119

Chapter 9: The Masonic College of Kentucky 139

Chapter 10: Trip to the Holy Land 153

Chapter 11: The 19th Century Poet Laureate of Freemasonry 165

Chapter 12: Later Years and Eternal Life 179

Appendix A 193

References 197

About the Author 203

Acknowledgments

This revised edition of A Place in the Lodge: Dr. Rob Morris, Freemasonry and the Order of the Eastern Star was written to celebrate the 200th birth anniversary of Rob Morris who was born on August 31, 1818. Dr. Paul Rich and Westphalia Press are thanked for making this possible. Their enthusiasm and assistance was much appreciated. Included in this edition are more letters and images as well as additional research on Morris' writings.

Mariam Touba, Reference Librarian, Patricia D. Kingenstein Library, The New York Historical Society located the work records and site locations for Rob Morris' father, Robert Shaw Peckham.

Dr. Robert Fitch (1934-2013), Great grandson of Dr. Rob Morris, provided stories and information about the Morris' father.

Bonita Hilmer, an Internet researcher, provided records on Rob Morris' brother, John Anson Peckham and clarified the birthplace of the Peckham children in New York City. Her internet records were of great assistance.

J. B. Hitt, II, a Rob Morris descendent, provided Internet research.

Lucien Rule (1898-1964), an Oldham County historian and friend of Rob Morris, was a great resource for establishing a timeline and life history of Morris.

Barbara Manley Edds was of great assistance at the Rob Morris Historic Home in LaGrange, Ky.

Andrew Boisvert of the Old Colony Historical Society, Taunton, Massachusetts helped locate Morris School records.

Darlene Roberts, Grand Secretary of Order of the Easter Star in Mississippi, Terry Nowell, caretaker of the Little Red Schoolhouse (Eureka Masonic College), and Claude "Bubber" William Carnathan, OES and Trustee for the Little Red Schoolhouse, provided assistance with local lodge history of the Little Red Schoolhouse.

Mickie McMann, Grand Secretary of the Grand Lodge of Mississippi, assisted with the location of Lodge memberships for Rob Morris when Morris lived in Mississippi.

Thomas Savini, Chancellor Robert R. Livingston Masonic Library, Masonic Library of the Grand Lodge, New York City.

Karen Marshal-King, OES of New York State, provided assistance on Clara Barton records.

Linda Holman, Trustee of the Rob Morris Memorial Home, helped with access to the home and records.

Livingston Masonic Library for the Grand Lodge of New York and the Scottish Rite Masonic Museum and Library in Lexington, Massachusetts were invaluable resources. Raymond Dotson's website featured various aspects of Rob Morris' life.

The Department of Archives and History in Jackson Mississippi helped with research in locating information on the Eureka Masonic College.

Jessica Theiss Gray is acknowledged for her final edits and help on this manuscript.

Michael E. "Mike" Berry, Right Worthy Grand Treasurer and Right Worthy Grand Trustee Emeritus, General Grand Chapter, Order of the Eastern Star assisted with some final edits on the manuscript and updated information on the General Grand Chapter, Order of the Eastern Star.

Introduction

This book was written about the life of Rob Morris (1818-1888) based on a collection of over 200 letters composed by Morris and members of his family. The letters were salvaged by Marjorie Morgan Applegate and her first husband Davis "Zeke" Morgan. Marjorie and Zeke, both members of Masonic orders, cared for Ethel Morris, whose husband, LeRoy Morris, was the great-grandson of Dr. Rob Morris. The letters had been passed down through the family line. When Morris began these letters with his wife, Charlotte, he instructed her to save and bind the letters so they could read them in their old age.

The letters in this collection were transcribed by the author and, for the most part, kept in their original vernacular and vocabulary. The misspellings that were kept, gave context and insight to the character and background of the people who wrote the letters. The collection of letters, now property of the Grand Chapter of Kentucky, Order of the Eastern Star, are insightful on Morris' life and decisions as he shifted his career from teacher to traveling salesman to Masonic lecturer. The letters begin in 1847 and end in 1860 when the Morris family finally settled into a permanent home in LaGrange, Ky.

Morris' early years, as he pursued his Masonic career while trying to support his wife and young children, provided a perspective about travel, family relationships, and day-to-day life in the antebellum south. Many of the issues regarding education, the women's movement, pioneer living, and the widening fracture between the northern and southern states are reflected in the family letters.

Rob Morris' contributions to the Order of the Eastern Star (OES), an androgynous fraternity that embraced both men and women into the Masonic circle, are still revered today. This was one of the first national organizations for women that gave them a voice on local and national issues. The OES helped frame many of the issues raised when the "Declaration of Sentiments" (1848) was created that gave women more opportunities in education, jobs, and entitlements. Since Lucien Rule's book *Pioneering in Masonry: The Life and Times of Rob Morris* (1922), little had been published about Morris' life. The family letters clarified some of the questions regarding Morris' life such as his birthplace, how he organized the OES, his relationships with his siblings and his involvement with slavery.

Morris was a prolific writer and produced poetry, wrote Masonic journals, articles, and books. He produced poems for special events such as cornerstone dedications, funerals, and Masonic gatherings. This talent won him the title as Poet Laureate for Freemasonry in the 19th Century (Scottish poet, Robert Burns, held the title for the 18th Century.) Morris believed masons could provide educational opportunities for youth and women that made society a better place. He believed that Masonic principles were deeply embedded in century-old rituals that could only improve society's condition for future generations.

Rob Morris at age 54. Courtesy of *The Grand Chapter of Kentucky, Order of the Eastern Star (OES)*.

Cover of bound letters that were sewn together by wife Charlotte.
Courtesy of the Grand Chapter of Kentucky, OES.

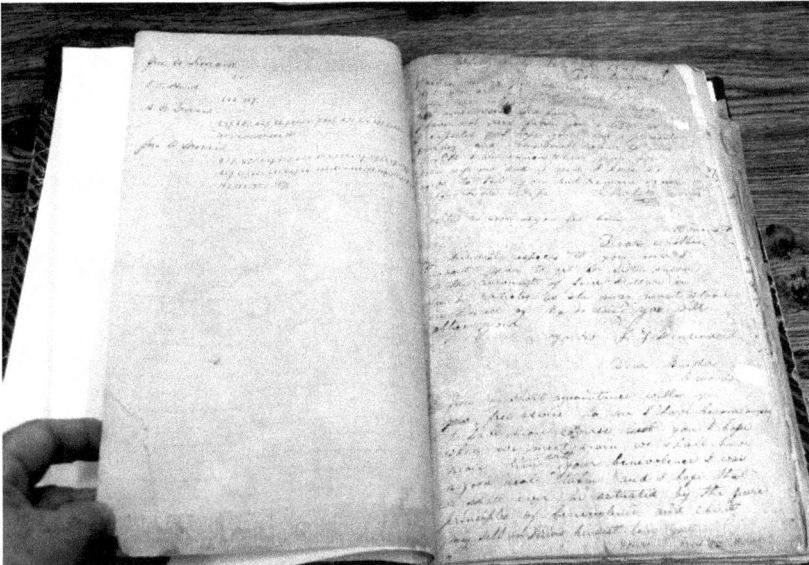

Inside look at a bound letter from the Rob Morris Collection used
for this book. *Courtesy of the Grand Chapter of Kentucky, OES.*

CHAPTER ONE

Childhood, Brother John, and Sister Charlotte

As with all historic figures, there are errors and misconceptions that occur over time and the figure of Rob Morris is no different. For example, there was speculation about Rob Morris' birth and early years with confusion over his birthplace and where he spent his youth. Some records and information indicated Morris was born in Taunton, Massachusetts and that he was apprenticed out at an early age to the John Morris family, where he adopted the "Morris" surname. Other sources said that he was highly educated with degrees in medicine and/or law, presumably during his apprenticeship years. There were also indications he had little or no connections with his sister and brother. The family letters helped clarify those relationships.

Rob Morris' parents were Robert Peckham (1789-1825) and Charlotte Lavinnia Shaw (1786-1837). Robert and Charlotte married in Taunton, Massachusetts on December 1, 1811. Peckham and Shaw were of English and Scottish descent whose families settled in Rhode Island and Massachusetts. With surnames of Peckham, Fales, Little and Paine, Robert Peckham's ancestors were some of the first pilgrims arriving in New England during the early to mid-1600s (Hillmer, 2014).

Charlotte Lavinnia Shaw's family were mariners. Her father, John Shaw, was a sea captain who traveled back and forth to the West Indies. John Shaw built a house in the Taunton area where he and his wife, Hannah Keith Shaw, lived. John died in 1821, but Charlotte's mother, Hannah, outlived Charlotte by two years.

Charlotte and Robert Peckham had five children. The first two, John Fales Peckham and Mary Shaw Peckham, died in infancy. The third child, John Anson was born in 1816 followed by Robert Peckham (Morris) in 1818, and sister Charlotte Fales Peckham in 1821. All three children were born in New York City where their father Robert, worked as an accountant at 99 Greenwich. In a listing from the city directory in 1818, the home address for Peckham and his wife is 26 Rector Street. From the same directory, a William McKenny is listed working at a marble yard located at 99 Greenwich and living at 24 Rector Street. This indicated a relationship between Peckham and McKenny working at a marble yard and situated as neighbors. In subsequent years, the listing for Peckham changed to 24 Greenwich (Longworth, 1818.)

In 1821, the couple split and Charlotte left her husband and returned to Taunton, taking their infant daughter, Charlotte Fales, with her. The two boys, John and Robert were left to live with their father in NYC. On Feb. 2, 1825, Robert Peckham died at a NYC hospital and John and Robert went home to live with their mother. Baptism records show that Charlotte baptized her children, John, Robert, and Charlotte Fales, on May 14, 1826 at the Pilgrim Congregational Church in Taunton. In the same year, Charlotte Shaw Peckham married Silas Shepherd. Charlotte died 11 years later on Dec. 31, 1837 (Compton, n.d.).

Recently, archivist Andrew Boisvert, at the Old Colony Historical Society in Taunton, Massachusetts ran across student records from the Bristol Academy for Robert W. Peckham. The records show that Morris was enrolled from 10 years of age until 16 years at the Academy in the Fall 1828, Spring 1829, Fall 1829, Spring 1832, and Spring 1834. During this time, Rob Peckham changed his surname from Peckham to Morris and gave little information about his surname change, but stated in later years that "I adopted the apparently quaint and odd cognomen of *Rob* as a prefix. The immediate cause of this was my determination not any longer to be confounded with the author Robert Morris from New York (Dotson, 1984)."

In the following excerpt of a letter, Rob Morris indicated to his son, John that he left home from New York at age 18:

Louisville, Sept. 19, 1852

My Dear Little Boy

Last Tuesday the Whigs had a great time celebrating General Scott's entrance into the city of Mexico. The cannons roared and the trumpets sounded and the bells rang. They had a great barbecue at which twenty thousand people ate their dinner

On Wednesday the Democrats had a barbecue but it rained hard. On Thursday was your birthday and you were nine years old. Only think of it, nine years old. Why in nine more years you will be as old as I was when I left New York and went away off to Illinois to keeping school. You will be as tall and big as I am now. I don't care much about your being tall and big but I want you to be a good man. Nobody can be a happy man unless he is a good man.

It is raining here today so that folks cannot go to meeting so much as they would like to. Does Robert talk about Pa much? Oh how I should like to take him on one arm and little Sarah on the other and go six times round the house while sister and Alfred follow us and all would be happy.

From a diary entry July 1848 from Wheeling, West Virginia, on his way to New York City Morris wrote:

> It was here in 1839 and took the same road that I am to take tomorrow. This is the same house that I ate a Christmas dinner in when old Felix Grundy was here with me. I was then a young man and he an old one. He is dead and I am here with nine years more on   my heart and my heart with my little wife and three children far off in Tennessee. I get mighty anxious to come home when I sit here in my lonely chamber and think about you all.
>
> From Your Father.

Morris' reference to "keeping school in Illinois" indicated his job as a head-master. Private schools were organized in pioneer communities as west-ward expansion was rapidly advancing. Headmasters were sought to teach at this private seminaries and job opportunities were available for young men like Morris, who could demonstrate they had received a basic educa-tion (Hamlett, 1914.)

Felix Grundy mentioned in one of the letters, was a politician and attorney, born in Virginia, educated in Kentucky who settled his later years in Ten-nessee. His expansive career included terms in Kentucky at the House of Representatives, the Court of Appeals, and as Chief Justice. He also served as United States Senator from Tennessee. He was the Attorney General in President Martin Van Buren's Cabinet and was known as mentor to a future president, James K. Polk. Four counties in Tennessee were named for Felix Grundy (United States Congress, 2014.)

Morris traveled to Grundy's Tennessee and found a job close to Memphis where he met his future wife, Charlotte Mendenhall. From Memphis, Mor-ris sought other career opportunities and moved his family several times in Mississippi, Tennessee, and southwestern Kentucky until 1859 when they settled in their permanent home at LaGrange, Ky.

Rob Morris and his sister, Charlotte Fales Peckham Wilson and brother, John Anson Peckham

Rob's brother and sister continued to influence his family and life well after he left the East coast. He named his children after them, he visited them often throughout his journeys back East for Masonic affairs and he took his son John on a trip to meet Aunt Charlotte and Uncle John in 1850. The following letters are taken out of context from the rest of the chapters in this book for several reasons. They did not "fit" the sequence of events as with the other letters, but they gave proof of his deep ties to his brother and sister that continued throughout his life. The letters also gave insight about Morris' childhood which revealed undertones of an abusive father that may have influenced the decision to go West.

Charlotte Fales Peckham Wilson

Rob's sister, Charlotte (1821-1903), maintained a warm and loving relationship with both her brothers. She was the contact that kept the brothers in touch with each other as well as kept both of them aware of their family relationships and status. Charlotte's letters and handwriting indicated that she was well educated. Barely a few months old when her parents separated in New York City, Charlotte's mother retreated to Taunton with Charlotte, a babe in arms, leaving the two boys with their father. Charlotte was the second wife of Dr. Elisha Tyson Wilson (1813-1874) when they married on April 11, 1849. Dr. Wilson, a dentist, lost his first wife shortly after the birth of their fourth child in 1848. Children from the first marriage were Eugene, Charles, Cecil, and Ella. Records indicated that only three children survived their father (New England Historical and Genealogical Register, 1875, p. 204.)

Dr. Wilson was a prominent citizen in Boston, a Mason and Knights Templar. He served as a City Alderman during 1861-1862 and became Chief Executive Officer of the Soldiers Fund after the Civil War. This fund was a relief fund for the veterans. He, along with one of his colleagues, Dr. Parker, helped to establish in 1867 the American Academy of Dental Science. Charlotte never remarried after Wilson's death and she died in 1903, at their Boston home. Both she and her husband are buried in Taunton (Ibid.)

John Anson Peckham

There were only two years difference in age between brother John (1816-1865) and Rob as they spent their early childhood years together with their father in New York City. In adult life, a military record shows that a John A. Peckham was enlisted in the 154 N.Y. Infantry, Company C. with rank in 1861 as "musician" and mustered out in 1864 as "musician." He married Susan Harrod Metcalf on July 7, 1847 at the St. Thomas Episcopal Church in Taunton. He was a Mason listed as the member of King David Lodge in Massachusetts (Taunton Genealogy, 2014.)

John and Susan had three daughters, Charlotte Lydia (b.1848), Susan Harrod (b.1849), and Anna Fales (b.1852.) The census records from Taunton in 1870 listed one of the daughters, Susan, as a music teacher. John died at age 49 leaving a young family for his wife to manage. From Charlotte's letters to Rob, she often discussed John's financial difficulties and his repeated return to a "low brow life with sinful friends." John moved from Massachusetts, New York, Chicago, St. Paul, and Louisville often leaving his family behind and in financial stress. Rob and John had a falling out for a period of time, but regained their relationship. There were a few times that Rob sent money to John's wife, Susan, to help with support. The circumstances of John's death in 1865 are not clear (Ibid.)

The first contact Rob made with his siblings, after he saw them last as a young man on his westward journey, was the summer of 1848 when he traveled northeast for business pursuits. The following letter is from Rob to wife Charlotte written from Taunton, Massachusetts, Sunday, July 23, 1848:

My Dear Charlotte

After so many years absence I am sitting here this morning at my brother's house. I arrived July 21 just before night and found John at home waiting for me. Charlotte did not get here until yesterday. Both are well and seem happy to meet their brother and to spend a week with him.

John is very comfortably situated in an excellent house, surrounded by friends with a good wife and pretty child which he seems very fond of. He is getting a salary of one thousand dollars a year and his employers seem to think a great deal of him and he of them. Charlotte has been spending six months in Boston and will return there as soon as I leave. She looks much better than the picture she sent us, her face is thin but good looking, her hair is very black. I think there is a great resemblance between her and our little girl and she appears to be determined to have little Sis and educate her as soon as she gets old enough.

I have not been to see an of my other relations yet but shall do so tomorrow and b gone from here two days.

I have been happier in this visit than I expected. John is the same generous kind hearted man he was twelve years ago and although he looks older than he did yet I can see the same features which used to smile upon me and hear the same voice which was the kindest to me in my youthful days. Charlotte is talkative and affectionate, reminding me of our dear mother and of the days when we played together as children so long ago.

We have taken a long walk together and we went this evening to the Methodist Church together and tomorrow we shall ride together.

In part I expect she will be with me all the time I am here.

You can perceive that I have every reason to enjoy my visit well. But one thing is absent which I could wish for that is my dear family, my wife and my children. With looking back to Tennessee and wishing I leave here so soon. You would be as welcome here as I am—all want to see you and love you.

John wants to see his namesake. I want to see four of you and with all these wants we sometimes forget to enjoy the pleasures we possess.

They were much disappointed because I did not bring your likenesses as I promised but I have consoled them by saying that I will try to get them before Christmas if I can get money enough to pay for them.

The serman this evening was What Shall I do to be Saved? The minister first told us what was meant by Salvation and proved to us that it was the most important thing we could ask for. Then he said if we would get salvation we must not grieve the Holy Spirit, we must not wait for more consideration, we must no dread the ridicule of the world. We must believe that we are great sinners, that we deserve external punishment, that Christ is able to help us that he is willing and we must give ourselves up to Him. My dear wife, d you feel your Salvation is safe with Jesus Christ, that you are devoted to him and expect to enjoy him in heaven. If you do then let the world see that you are a Christian. Act as nearly like Christ as you can. Pray for the assistance of the Holy Spirit and when you find that temptations are about to overcome you then commit yourself to God in prayer and you amy be sure that you will have strength given you to do a Christian duty.

Remember that our Savior suffered in silence.

He was patient and made no complaint although his cares were much greater than ours. He thought of us when he promised to send us the Holy Spirit for our Comforter and he will be always give that spirit when we pray for it.

May the grace of God be with you dear wife, and with your children.

May every happy hour we have passed together be so sanctified in your memory that every recollection of it may bring to you pleasure and satisfaction.

May we meet again soon, lie many pleasant years together in this world and then see Jesus in his everlasting hour.

Your husband R Morris

As Morris' Masonic career expanded he made repeated contacts with his siblings. In 1849 on one of his Masonic tours, he mentioned a visit to his brother and sister and brother-in-law when he traveled to New York:

New York, August 28, 1849

My Dear Wife

When I wrote to you last week I had not received any letter from you and was afraid you had not written. But your letter came and I got it and I am glad that I am permitted to hear that you are all in health. May the same kind Father who has watched over you thus far, continue to be your protector and support during my absence.

My own health is excellent. I am growing more fleshy every day and hope you will see quite a change in my appearance. I will call on you as you request and take you home with me. There is no place like home. But you must be all ready when I arrive, for I cannot stop more than a few hours. I am buying a great many books and other things to sell in Jackson. People seem willing to give me credit for whatever I want.

You did not say much about our children. Do they remember me yet? Are they happy at grandpa's? Be sure that John says his lessons every day and mind that he pays attention to what you tell him.

Tell John that Uncle Wilson has given me a beautiful gold pencil. Aunt Charlotte sent all the children some things. To sister, she sent a string of red coral beads. She gave me a beautiful picture of herself.

Mr. Wilson writes to me from Jackson every week. Things are getting on there pretty well.

The cholera is still in this city about thirty deaths a day but the city is so large that no body seems to miss the dead and not a word is said about the disease. People in these large towns are very cold hearted.

Be kind to my dear babies for their pa's sake and may god bless you all. Your true friend

R. Morris

Brother John expected an addition to his family some time this week. We were only together three hours.

Charlotte Morris Wilson maintained correspondence with Rob and his family throughout the years. She was very fond of her namesake, Rob's daughter Charlotte, and always wrote with love and affection as the following letters indicated.

Roxbury, Massachusetts, December 11, 1853

Your last letter my dear brother is not quite two months old-don't you think I am doing remarkably well to answer it so soon? The fact is nature blessed me with quite a large conscience and where you are concerned, it will not keep quiet after a certain length of time has elapsed, until I get out my pen and paper, and squire accounts with you. As it was just concerning its hints and suggestions "that" it was time Roberts letters were answered. I thought I would knock it in the head at once, and confront myself with the assurance that my debts were all discharged from a short time at best. So much for so much and now how do you do? All well, I trust—We have had a lovely autumn here, am even now the weather is as nice and balmy as Spring. As often winter is not usually a healthy one, but I cannot but rejoice, for the poor 's sake, that thus far this cold has been delayed. Full air provisions are so high there will be much suffering when the winter really lets in.

I congratulated you or rather your family that you have got back to the country again. If they dislike the city as much as I do, it must have been a real source of pleasure to leave it—and with children too. It is so much better to let them have a free range in the open air that to have them up in the close streets of a city. How often do you see them? That part of it I should object to, if I were you wife. She doubtless is willing to sacrifice her own personal wishes for the sake of the general good. I do hope success may wait upon your efforts so that in your old age, you may lay aside your oars, and enjoy the fruits of your hard labors—"Give me neither riches nor poverty"—

I passed Thanksgiving at John's—had a very pleasant time—I still hope we may able be together on some future day, to enjoy this good old New England festival but God only knows. I believe it was celebrated in Kentucky on the same day it was here—of course you were at home. I had quite a treat while there, in receiving a package of letters by our Father and Mother during the first years of their marriage to Uncle O'Brien Shaw—Aunt Sarah sent them to us and a valuable gift they were. John and I divided them but you shall have your share when you come to see us. They date back to 1810- speak of Mary Falis' birth and many interesting family matters. Dear Mother, this season of the year is always filled with meaning—a recollection of her—her sickness and death particularly. I had a dream of her not long since which bought her so vividly to mind. I could hardly dismiss myself of the idea that she was still living—so plainly did I see her that when I awoke, it was some time before I could realize that it was only in dreams that I should ever see her again. Dear Mother, I shall never forget her— never cease to mourn her.

I believe I am in Johnnie's debt, in respect to letters—but he must not let the correspondence cease because I am not punctual. Let him write whenever he is inclined—I shall always be glad to hear from him, and will reply as frequently as I can.

And my little Charlotte too, are not her pat looks eligible yet? Remember her first effusion is to be mine—Is she growing pretty? The sweet face quite haunts me as I am looking forward to the time when she will be under my care with a great deal of pleasure. How is the lump of fat, you call your baby—Tell your wife they exhibit monsters at the museum here at very good rates, and if you get short of funds, I'll undertake the exhibition at a very reasonable commission. Kiss the whole tribe for me from Johnnie down. What a sweet little fellow he must be—don't work him to hard-remember children love play and Jack will be a dull boy, if he has too much to do—

We are still boarding in Roxbury. The doctor is succeeding as well as be expected. His practice increased slowly but I hope surely —we expect to be at housekeeping in the Spring but cannot tell yet—He sends love to one and all. Smile whenever you can. Good bye with a heart full of love to you and your better half. I am   always your loving

Sister Charlotte

In the next letter, Charlotte updated her brother on family affairs and John's business affairs and discussed Susan, John's wife.

To: Robert Morris, Hickman, Fulton Co., Kentucky

Roxbury, Feb. 25, 1854

I have been waiting for the letters you wished my dear brother, before writing you. Susan sent them down a few days since and I do not doubt you will be as much interested in them as I was. If you wish to retain any of them, do so, and the remainder you can return whenever you choose. I have been in Taunton for a day or two during the last week. Stayed one night with Susan. John is in New York, looking up business. He has left Mr. Mason and hoped to find something to do in New York. Poor John, he has had some sad experiences in the course of his life and I fear may meet with many more. He never has and never will learn economy and no one can live many years spending more than their income without feeling the effects, and in his case, very severely. I know nothing definitely of his affairs. I only know he is in trouble and my heart ached for him and his family. If he had but the comforts and consolations of the gospel to sustain him in the hour of his adversity all would be well. But he cares not for them. My prayer to God for him is not for worldly prosperity but that these, his trials, may bring him low at the foot of the cross and that he may find those riches which are just and may not corrupt and which thieves can not break through and steal—He will doubtless inform you of his plans when they are full matured.

We are all well and have been through the winter and such a winter it has been. I believe it has gone all over our land so I presume you have had a portion of it in Kentucky—the cold and snow. I mean the storms here have been frightful and the cold intense. Then, too, the provisions and fuel have been so high that much suffering has existed among the poor classes. Indeed it is a mystery to me how they have lived at all. We have been very comfortably situated- are still boarding—it is doubtful if we go to housekeeping this Spring as thought I very much hope to. With your children and own house is decidedly the pleasanter place.

I have no reason to complaint, for we have had every comfort we could have asked for. Business is still encouraging if we can weather through the coming year with God's permission I think our darkest days will be over.

American Freemason

ROB. MORRIS, Editor.

J. F. BRENNAN, Publisher.

"If the foundations be destroyed, what can the righteous do?"

VOL. III.   LOUISVILLE, KY : DECEMBER 1, 5851.   NO. 5.

Masonic Jurisprudence.

REPLIES TO QUERIES ON MASONIC JU-RISPRUDENCE.

The *American Freemason* was a newspaper edited and written in part by Morris, to provide guidance and standardization of rituals for local lodges during the Conservator Period of Morris's work. one of the several newspapers that were written by Rob Morris.

Shall you not be on this Spring? I want to see you so much. I rather hope you will not come, until we have a house to put you in. Then come and stay as long as you will. I am glad to hear such good accounts of the children- hope they are all well now. As for your poor wife, she is a perfect martyr. Why she'll never live through such frequent additions to her family—Poor soul, tell her my heartfelt sympathy is hers.

How is it about my correspondence with Master Johnnie? Which he in debt? I presume it is myself for he is so prompt, he never would have let so long a time pass without reply to a letter but tell him he must not wait for me to answer every letter but write, whenever he is inclined and I'll not entirely forget him. Miss Lottie too is old enough to open as communication is she not? I want to know of her progress in learning and can judge better in that way than any other. Give much love and kisses to them all. The Doctor is quickly smoking his cigar and takes a breath to send kind remembrances. Write soon—do

Good-bye yours fondly, Charlotte.

Rob provided numerous work opportunities for John over the years including a move to Louisville as indicated in the following.

Louisville, Kentucky, March 29, 1854

My Dear Wife,

I got back from New York this morning after a pleasant visit there of nine days. John came back with me and is here now. I think he will conclude to move his family here after a while. He is in good health and would like to see you very much. I found that his prospect in Massachusetts were tolerably good but though he would do better here and so I persuaded him to come. My health is very good and prospect of business good. Tomorrow I shall go down to Owensboro to commence lecturing. Next Sunday I will write you a long letter also one to John.

your dear husband, Rob

Rob paid his brother to sell subscriptions for Masonic journals. Charlotte, as the family matriarch, always lamented about their brother's lifestyle who became her constant source of worry. *(Author's note: Lasie is the nickname for John's wife, Susan.)*

Boston, March 6, 1855

Your letter my dear brother has been too long unanswered- the truth is my husband has no time but the evening to himself and then he is too tired for anything and I have been waiting until I could tell you that the money you requested for John, had been forwarded to his wife. I can now do so—she had received it and the insurance policy is safe for another year. It was a difficult matter for the Dr. to obtain the funds for ready money is a commodity very rare in these regions and for no other purpose would he have made the effort—I could not urge him for I knew he has debts which that same money ought to have settled. But as I said before the business is now satis-factorily arranged and no one can rejoice more than I—that is so. I am truly thankful to hear such good accounts of John. May the Lord bless him and strengthen him in his endeavors. I have always had a strong feeling that he would eventually be brought to see things in a very different light from what he has ever done. And although he may be humbled to the very dust before this end he attained, he will yet give thanks that he had been afflicted. Yea even tho his own sins have wrought the affliction.

Lasie was down last week and passed a night with me. She keeps up good courage that all looked very dark to her. She has proven her-self a true noble woman and John, while he possesses her can never feel wholly deserted. She is to have another boarder soon and then with what you are to pay John, I see no reason why they may not b e very comfortable. I hope you will be able to pay regularly, his stipulat-ed sum, and then Spring may open with brighter days for your both.

It has been a hard winter for every one—had it not been for our boarders I do not know how we should have weather the storm. Business is good with the Dr. but payments are very slow and our expenses are very great.

How are the babies and your good wife? I shall enclose this to John, for you did not say where you should be.

Write soon, do—what has become of the European trip?

Love and kisses to all—tell Johnnie he owed me a letter I be-lieve—at any rate— he must write the next one.

Elisha sends love- good bye—yours ever fondly, Charlotte

In the next letter, Charlotte indicated her distress that Rob and John have separated ways. She also congratulated Rob's family on the birth of Ruth Electa.

Boston, Sept. 10, 1855

Dear Robert

Why have we not heard from you since you left here? Johnnies letter gave a very minute account of your journey home and of the new member of your family. Accept my congratulations and don't give Miss Ruth Electa too much potato to eat if you wish her to live—

Do tell me, what finally caused the rupture between you and John. I can learn nothing distinctly from him. He is now in New York—doing nothing and writes home in the most doleful manner to his wife. I do not know what will become of him or his family. Susan is in miserable health and altho she heard up as well as you could expect I am afraid will not much longer endure the anxiety she has had the last two years.

Write soon do—shall you be on this fall? The Dr. sends love— he is very busy, but is going to try to go to the great mason's meeting in Philadelphia where he hopes to meet you.

In sleepiness but much love, your ever, Charlotte

Continued correspondence by Charlotte indicated a continued separation between Rob and John. John and Susan eventually moved to Minnesota. The following are the last two letters in this collection written by Charlotte to Rob.

Boston, Sept 19, 1859

My Dear Brother

I was absent from home when your letter arrived. I have only re-turned a week since so that I have had no time to reply to it until now.

I am so sorry to hear of your illness but hope you had no draw-backs and are not quite yourself again. I could easily imagine that you would need an introduction to yourself after a three week visitation of fever and fatigue. I trust you have filled up the hollows of your face and are now so far like your former self that I should recognize you were you to become visible on Tremont St.

I passed nearly a month in Taunton this summer and enjoyed it very much. Part of the time I was at Oakland where visions of the past came up before me and brought back to my memory thoughts of her who has so long ago lived and died there but whose image is as fresh in my heart as it was the day she was taken from us. Dear Mother! How many tears I have shed for her and yet I have never seen the hour when I would have called her back.

Aunt Betsey is still living but is a terrible sufferer. She was very low when I first saw her and entirely unconscious but rallied again and the day before I left I went to enquire about her. I found her quite comfortable and delighted to see me. She asked for you and John and sent her love. It is wonderful how her strength holds out. I only hope she may not be left to linger for years. As her own Mother did, losing her mind and becoming a burden to herself and those around her.

Father Shepard is very feeble and has grown to be an old man. He is very deaf, has lost all his teeth and the sight of one eye but still attends to his business and his mind is as clear as ever.

I hear every week or so from lt. Paul and have pleasant cheerful letters.

By this time you have probably had the expected addition to your family. I hope you are both resigned but I also hope it will be the last for I think you have done your share.

The Dr. had a very pleasant trip to Niagara but was sorry not to see you there. He wished to add a few lines to this so I will leave him to tell his own story.

Give lots of love to Mama and all the chicks including the newcomer. Let me hear from you very soon again.

Ever your affectionate sister, Charlotte.

Boston, Nov. 13, 1859

I have just finished a letter to Susan dear Robert, telling her about dear old Aunt Betsey's death and supposing it will be equally as interesting to you. I will give you too an account of the last hours of one, who while still living, loved us all so well. She has been growing weaker and weaker for many months. Indeed it was surprising to all who saw her how long life lasted in so frail a tenement.

I saw her in September and thought that she could not survive many days. She was delighted to see me, inquired for John and you and sent messages of love to you both. She lingered along until last week, lot times suffering much, and then again rallying when she grew rapidly worse, having a constant succession of the terrible convulsions she has had all through her sickness until Friday heaving when she died. The last few hours of her life she received free from pain but as thought speechless,Virginia thought she knew her. Her last audible words were to call each of her children by name and then faintly murmur "heaven". I rejoiced when I heard she had gone— gone where all her cares, her pains, her sorrows are over. Washed in her Saviour's blood, clothed in his righteousness she had entered upon her rest "that rest that remaineth- for the people of God". She was buried by her husband's side on the old burial ground on the plain and a large number of friends followed her remains to their final resting place. Her life was one of quiet devotion to her duties- nothing brilliant marked it, but "his works do follow her" and I verily believe she is now reaping her reward in Paradise. May we so live that we shall meet her there.

The little money that Uncle Alfred left will now be divided one half of the whole and the rest to be equally shared by the other daughters. I suppose there will be about $2000.

I heard of you through Dr. Lewis who said he met you in Chicago. You were looking badly according to his accounts on this. I hope you have quite recovered and are well and strong again, Charlotte too. I trust had got up her sickness and about exercising the oversight and authority necessary in so large a household as yours. Did she mourn for her little one? I always feel that an infant is spared so much when it is taken away from earth and it had drank of its bitter cup that I can rejoice for them.

But I have never been called upon to give up one of my own and therefore I cannot sympathize as others might. The grief would have been greater for you both if it had been either of the other children and time will soon soother the parting death must always bring when it takes away one who is bone of our bone and flesh of our flesh.

We are all well. The Dr. grows a little with dyspepsia but on the whole is in good condition. When shall we see you? I hope you have written to Minnesota. I have pleasant accounts from them frequently.

Give love and many kisses to the children for me. Alfred's letters seem suddenly to have ceased—what's the trouble? Goodbye, fondly your sister, Charlotte.

CHAPTER 2
Love, Marriage, and Family

Rob Morris took advantage of the numerous job opportunities open for teachers at small academies as he ventured west. One such job was at the DeSoto Academy in northwestern Mississippi, a few miles from Germantown, Shelby County, Tennessee outside Memphis. There he met his future wife, Charlotte Mendenhall. Charlotte and Rob were married on May 26, 1841 in Shelby County (Hillmer, 2014.) Over the course of their marriage, they produced eight children.

Charlotte Mendenhall Morris and Family

Charlotte's parents were Samuel and Sarah Mendenhall. Census records show the Mendenhalls lived in Limestone, Alabama before moving to Shelby, County, Tennessee. Samuel's brother, Isaac, lived in Shelby County and Sam moved his family to be close to brother Isaac and for job opportunities. Most of their five children, including Charlotte (1818-1893) were born in Alabama. Charlotte's siblings were Sarah Ann (b. 1822), Jefferson G. (b. 1824), Poleta Jane (b. 1826), and Francis (b. 1830.)

Charlotte was close to her family and visited them often, sometimes boarding and living with family in Shelby County as her husband traveled the country. The Morris children often spent several days with their Mendenhall grandparents. Charlotte's brother, Francis, helped to build Rob and Charlotte's home in Fulton, County, Kentucky where they moved in 1852.

As Rob's career changed from schoolteacher to salesman to Masonic lecturer, Rob spent months at a time away from his young family. Charlotte cared for the children and managed the household. In January 1848, Rob set out to sell subscriptions for newspapers and magazines. He left Charlotte at home with three small children; John age five, Charlotte age three, and Alfred was eight months. Along with child rearing, there were years when yellow fever, whooping cough, measles, mumps, dysentery, and cholera plagued small villages and communities. Rob and Charlotte with their children were exposed to all of the diseases at one time or another.

Charlotte's basic reading, writing, and math were elementary at best. Under Rob's tutelage and encouragement, she worked to improve her skills. She became the teacher for the children getting instructions from Rob in the regular correspondence between them during his travels.

Mt. Sylvan Academy

In 1842, Robert and Charlotte moved to vicinity of the Oxford, Mississippi, where they had their first child, Robert Samuel Morris who died within the year. They had their second son, John Anson Morris on Sept. 17, 1843. On May 12, 1845 their first daughter, Charlotte Fales Morris was born. In 1845, Rob became president and professor of Mt. Sylvan Academy (near Burgess, Mississippi) a year before he "came into the light" of Freemasonry. In his autobiography, Morris described Mt. Sylvan as follows:

> I was Principal of Mount Sylvan Academy, an institution of learning established the year previous, some twelve miles west of Oxford, on the premises of a large-hearted mason and most worthy citizen, Honorable James Brown. Adjoining the school grounds was a plantation, the property of honorable Jacob Thompson, a distinguished politician of the day, and subsequently Secretary of the Interior under President Buchanan. Near this lay the homestead of honorable Isaac N. Davis, a gentleman of learning and leisure, afterwards of note in the Grand Lodge of Mississippi. Mr. Thompson, though not a mason at the time, was afterward initiated in the same Lodge with myself. Besides these there was but little society in the rather dreary "black-jack" hills which surrounded the Academy.

> It was quite a task for the school master, at the best not very strong in his physique, to ride on horseback twelve miles to Lodge and return in time for early morning recitation. Yet never appeared the way so short to me or the surroundings less somber upon my return home than was that Spring morning, after the ceremony (of initiation into freemasonry) before the mocking birds had returned from the South or more than a stray violet or two had appeared on the hillsides (Rule, 1922, p. 225.)

On March 5, 1846 at Gathright Lodge No. 33 in Oxford, Mississippi, Honorable James M. Howry, past grand master and high priest of Mississippi initiated the 28-year-old Morris into freemasonry (Grand Secretary, 1846, p. 67.) Howry was a district judge in Mississippi and was Rector at the University of Mississippi at Oxford. Morris reflected on that moment in later years:

Rob and Charlotte Morris during their earlier years of marriage.
Courtesy of The Grand Chapter of Kentucky, OES.

Charlotte's family, The Mendenalls, settled in Germantown near Memphis.

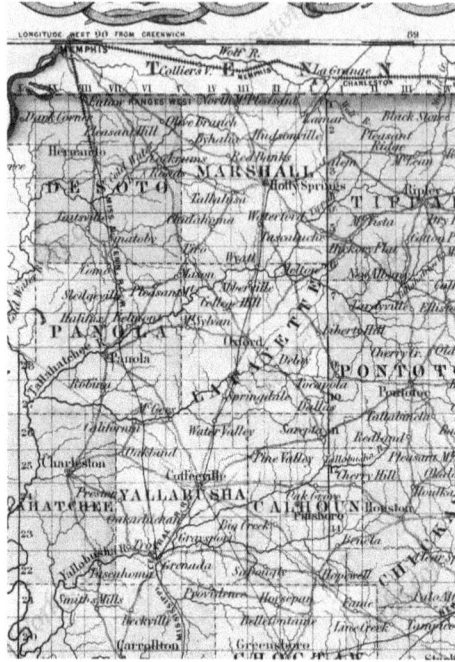

This map shows Mt. Sylvan Academy where Morris taught, located approximately 12 miles west from Oxford, Mississippi.

Prominent politician and businessman Jacob Thompson owned the plantation where the Sylvan Academy was located. His home, located in Oxford, Ms., is a historic site.

The University of Mississippi was founded by Masons from the Gathright Lodge, during the time and where Morris "came into the light of Freemasonry." The Lyceum, (pictured) completed in 1848, is currently the Administration Building.

The Shegoogs were friends of the Morris's and lived across the street from Jacob Thompson. Their home was later owned by novelist William Faulkner who named the home Rowan Oak and is now a historic site.

My first view of masonry was had on the evening of March 5, 1846. It was in the southwest corner jury room (upper story) of the old court house, in Oxford, LaFayette County, Mississippi. The night of my initiation was cold and raw—the room was open and in disrepair—the attendance was scanty—the adornments of the lodge were in the highest degree shabby and mean; but that first view of Masonic symbolism gave me a pleasure which sixteen years of similar sight-seeing has steadily increased. The first glance, the first explanation, the kind friend who stood before me, his warm and loving grip, (well I knew that Master as both loving and kind)—these were enough. In an instant I thereby gathered the genuine secret of masonry (op. cit., p. 224.)

In later years, Morris dedicated the Ninth Volume of the Universal Masonic Library to Howry: "No man has ever exercised more influence upon my mind that Judge Howry" (op. cit., p. 226.) Judge James Moorman Howry was well respected and admired. Born in 1804 in Fincastle Virginia, Howry began his law practice in Nashville, Tennessee where he served as Colonel in the Tennessee militia. Around 1836, Howry moved to Oxford, Mississippi where he served as Judge in the 8th Judicial District. He was a founding member of the University of Mississippi Board Of Trustees in 1844 and served until 1870. He served as state senator (1858-1861) and became the trustee of the Union Female College which later became the Oxford Female Academy under the Cumberland Presbyterians. Howry was a good friend of Jefferson Davis who corresponded with Howry frequently on matters of politics and governance (Hexon, Meg & Staff 2012.)

Howry and his wife, Narcissa Bowen (1818-1870) had several children, one of which, James Henry Howry married Mary Buena Vista Burney. Burney's father, the Reverend Dr. Stanford Guthrie Burney (1814-1893) was a mason and Cumberland Presbyterian who moved from Memphis to accept the position of President of Mt. Sylvan Academy in 1848 soon after Morris resigned his tenure there. Burney became friends with Howry and established the Union Female College at Oxford making Howry a trustee. Howry solicited Burney to become professor of English Literature as well as chair of the metaphysics department at the University of Mississippi.

Charlotte's family, the Mendenhalls, were friends of the Burneys who lived in the Memphis/Germantown area before moving to Oxford. From correspondence between Rob and Charlotte during subsequent years, Rob mentioned Mary Burney and her family when he visited Oxford, and Mary's inquiry about Charlotte and the children. Burney, in particular, encouraged Morris' interest in geology and they worked together to establish a geographical survey of Mississippi (see Chapter 3.)

The Morris family expanded with the birth of their third child, Alfred Williams Morris on April 3, 1847. Rob was dissatisfied with the meager wages of a headmaster at Mt. Sylvan and wanted to explore other career possibilities. In addition, he mentioned that he had health issues. One of the career possibilities for Morris was selling magazine and newspaper subscriptions. People living in the piney woods of the south were eager for news from "back East." News from back home in the more civilized big cities provided a connection of civility and etiquette for families that often lived miles apart. Trends in fashion, gossip, and politics were of interest and intrigue. By the end of the year, Morris was convinced he could support his family by starting a subscription business. He would travel from village to village in Mississippi, taking subscriptions for newspapers and magazines on topics that ranged from religion and politics to fashion and lifestyle.

Charlotte and the children left Oxford and moved back to Charlotte's family in Shelby County Tennessee. With Rob travelling, Charlotte could find help for childrearing by living close to her family. Often letters included diary entries as in the following from Rob to Charlotte that indicated a future of separations as Rob tidied up his tenure from Mt. Sylvan.

Mount Sylvan, November 11, 1847

My dear wife

I begin today to write you a letter. I expect to write a little every day. I am absent from you and I want you to do the same to me. I will send the letter once a week so that you will always hear from me no matter what part of the world I am in.

Keep my letters whole and once a year sew together so if I should live a few years you would have quite a book and when I come home you and I will read together. I pray God to bless you and our dear children tonight. I feel very anxious about little Charlotte but hope she will recover and that I shall see her fat and rosy.

Friday Nov 12

The weather has cleared off so well that I hope you will finish your journey today. Mrs. Trigg and her baby are both sick. I have taken James Vineyard into my room and he sleeps in the place where you ought to be. The room is lonesome and I must go to writing to keep from getting low spirited.

Saturday, Nov. 13

Mr. Trigg got home last night and says he met you near Clear Creek and that you are well. This led me to thank God with much gratitude and has relieved my feelings greatly. Today Mr. McKay moved the desk and bookcase and my room begins to look quite empty.

Sunday, Nov. 14

Professor Brown got home about noon and says he met you on Friday about 10 miles from Memphis and that all were doing well. This makes my Sabbath day a happy one.

Monday, Nov. 14, 1847

Susan and her little girl are quite sick today. Mrs. Trigg and child are getting well.

Tuesday, Nov. 15, 1847

Mr. Hunt got home about 3 o'clock and brought your letter of good news. It is the first letter you ever wrote me but I hope it will not be the last by a hundred.

Wednesday, Nov. 16, 1847

Susan and her girl are better. Today Miss Shegoog from Oxford visited us. We have our prayer meeting tonight. George Herron is to be married tonight to a young lady named Bryan.

Thursday, November 17, 1847

A very rainy and disagreeable day. Tell Grundy to call at Parson Grazier's and I think he will find the box of books. I must now close this letter and have it ready for tomorrow's mail. The weather is changing very cold but I hope it will not affect your health, my dear Wife no the sweet little children. Your husband sends you a heart full of love tonight, do not forget him.

God bless you all, R. Morris

America was a new republic which embraced the rising middle class that valued education over wealth. Education reform was an issue during the Antebellum era expanding to include women. Traditional subjects of female academies shifted. Needlework, dancing, music, and classic French lessons were discarded and replaced with the more proficient lessons of knowledge for women that included grammar, writing, bookkeeping, history, and geography. Instruction was oral with an emphasis on repetition and memorization (Allen, 1996.)

These ideals were supported strongly by masons who saw education as a middle-class value, not to be reserved for the elite classes. As is expanded in Chapter Nine, masons supported academies for both boys and girls and were instrumental in the initiation of a public school system when practical in the more populated cities. Morris' support for education initiatives that included women was an essential part of his pedagogy. Without prejudice, he encouraged and supported his wife to expand her own repertoire of academics as well as become a tutor for their children. The following letter is an example of basic curricula from Antebellum America with a system of rewards, a flute in this case, and punishment, a slap on the hands. The corporal punishment suggested by Morris is to be tenderly followed by a gentle scold that the child understands the reasons for the reprimand.

Sunday, December 26, 1847

My Dear Charlotte

I sit down this morning to fill up another sheet in writing to you that I may have a letter ready to send up by the wagon tomorrow. What a great thing is letter writing. Next to being with you it is the pleasantest thing to me to tell you on a sheet of paper all about my affairs and how much I love you all.

The following is the plan I want you to pursue with John in addition to what I have written to you before. Begin on New Year's Day to teach him how to read by spending half an hour with him every day, never losing a day. Teach him first the vowels: a, e, i, o, u, w, y. Then the letters: b, d, p, q, s, t ,m, n. When he knows these well let him begin to read in the First Reader beginning at the first lesson and taking it all clean. After reading a lesson put out the words, a syllable at a time for him to spell. Be very particular in this part to see that he speaks every letter loud and plain, for on the way he begins depends his future correctness in pronouncing.

After the first month pick out some pretty piece of prose and let him get it by heart, a section every day. Maybe the Lord's prayer will be best to begin with. And here make him speak every word so yu can hear it two steps off. Make him speak slowly and distinctly. By this plan you can get him well started by the middle of March and I shall be able to attend the first examination of your school. By the first of March teach him the figures: 1,2,3,4,5,6,7,8,9,0. Get him a little slate and let him learn to make them neatly.

Teach him the stops: " , ;, :, ." . They are named comma, semicolon, colon, period. Make him hold his book right, his head up, his finger on the place. Have a regular time of day every morning to attend to him and don't let company or anything else but sickness prevent you from attending to him every day.

Make him learn to go to school with clean hands and face and try all you can to get him to love his half hour of study. This you can do if you will always go at it yourself with a smiling countenance and a cheerful voice. Encourage him and promise him as much as possible. Show him how much he learned yesterday and where he begun last week and how far he must go to before Pa comes.

Tell him I will buy him a little Flute as soon as he gets through the First Reader. Be patient yourself. You will often feel fretted by his carelessness and obstinacy and forgetfulness but don't show it. Don't' speak to him until you can speak mildly and whatever you do, never scold.

Whip him whenever it is necessary and do it with a stick on the inside of his hands, about three hard blows on each hand. But never strike him in anger, and never whip him before you tell him what his fault is and make him promise not to do so anymore.

After you have whipped him talk to him again with kindness and let him see that it pains your heart to have to hurt you dear little boy.

Call nine o'clock your school time and when he goes a visiting have him come back by school time and when you go anywhere to spend a day take his book with you if you will not yet get back by school time.

All this will be tiresome to you for a few weeks but after that you will like it and it will be a pleasure to you to watch his progress from page to page.

He will be your scholar and his respect for his mother will increase as he gets more and more knowledge from you. You will be rewarded for all this trouble by the time he can stand by your side and read you a chapter in the Testament. Your heart will rejoice in the knowledge of your children and by the time John had learned to read and write and cipher from you, you will commence upon little Charlotte with as much pleasure as I feel when I commence to read a good book for the first time.

I believe I have said enough on this subject. Act it out faithfully and many heaven's blessings crown your labors is the wish of your husband.

I will close my letter on this sheet by a little more advice about yourself.

Read at least three chapters in the Testament every day, that will take you through four times a year. On Sunday read at least 10 chapters beginning at the book of Genesis and taking it clean through the old Bible.

Pick out some good book to read every day, Mrs. Henman's Poems, or Letters to Mothers or something that you like better and even if it is hard at first it will soon become easy to you and you will be what I want you to be, fond of readying. I must now close.

You will hear from me almost every week and I shall hope to have good news to write you often.

Almighty Father preserve my dear family from danger and from sin and bring us together again in a good time for Jesus sake,

Amen
Your husband
R. Morris

While Rob was closing his office at Mt. Sylvan, Charlotte and the children moved to Shelby County Tennessee to be close to her family. The burden of raising the family and separation from her husband was overwhelming.

November 23, 1847

Dear husband

I set to inform you that we are all well. I began to feel vey anxious to see you. John says he would like to pa verry well. Charlotte is geting well. She has ben mending evry she left home. Alfred is growing finely.Think four weeks along time before I see you.

I am tolerably unsatisfied. I would like it better if you was here. Come as soon as the seesion it out. The family is all well but Francis he has the inflammatory rheumatism. Jane has a fine son but equal to Alfred. I want you to write to me when you will be here. I want hear from you. I have thought of over the time we parted at the mill. Tell susan that I often think of her. Rite to me when you will send my clothes and where you wil send them to. I want you to send the flat irons to me. I have nothing more to say at present but remain your true friend. Charlotte Morris

Give my best respects to Mrs. Trigg.

CHAPTER 3

Life in the Antebellum South

Living in the south and particularly along the Mississippi valley was pitted with serious health issues. Cholera and yellow fever were running rampant and both plagued the Morris family and neighborhoods in which they lived. Yellow fever, transmitted by mosquitoes, caused fever, headache, chills, back pain, loss of appetite, nausea, and vomiting and resulted in a 20% mortality rate. There were continued period of yellow fever epidemics between the 1700s and 1850s with the notable epidemic of 1853 that hit New Orleans resulting in 8,100 official deaths. The standard treatment at the time was quinine and in the following letters Rob suggested to Charlotte to continue her quinine treatments for yellow fever. Quinine had been used for the treatment of malaria but in later years was discovered to be ineffective for yellow fever. Initially, it was thought that yellow fever was transmitted through the air or by personal contact. It wasn't until the late 1800s that Dr. Carlos Finlay suggested the fever was transmitted by mosquitoes (Valso, 2014.)

Cholera was another disease of epidemic proportions during this period of history. At the time, cholera was thought not to be contagious. By the late 19th century, it was recognized as a disease spread by microscopic organisms that flourished in dirty water. As cities introduced cleaner water and sewage systems, cholera began to disappear. Several times, both Charlotte and Rob referred to deaths of neighbors and people they knew that died from cholera. Morris talked about the indifference of people to the disease when he visited New York City during a major epidemic (Harvard Open Library, 2012.)

The obstacles of disease along with the difficulties of pioneer living and travel on dirt roads are constantly reflected in the family's correspondence. In Charlotte's letters, issues of both providing for the children and keeping a household give great insight to the physical demands on a day-to-day basis for pioneer women. Women were often left alone to attend to household matters as men took jobs that kept them away for weeks and months at a time.

In Rob's letters, the obstacles he faced as he traveled were often life threatening such as the incident he described on the Bigbee River or the very real hazards of explosions that regularly occurred on steamboats. These circumstances that faced Charlotte and Rob were pitted against seasonal events such as periods of flooding or drought not to mention frequent house fires created from ill-constructed chimneys and improperly vented stoves.

Morris traveled primarily on his horse in Mississippi, but occasionally used rail. The railroad tracks connected major towns within states, but few went long distances. Trains were incredibly slow as described by Morris in one of the following entries. During his travels, Morris picked up a couple of business partners, Robert McKay and William McKee, to help with the subscription business. Both were fellow masons who became lifelong friends of Morris.

With the influential contacts made at Mt. Sylvan and the newly formed University of Mississippi, Morris pursued his interest in geology and metaphysics, primarily through Rev. Burney. Newly formed states, such as Mississippi, were interested in mapping geological features for economic ventures. Rev. Burney encouraged Morris to get involved in state legislature to form a geological department and Morris made frequent trips to the state capitol of Jackson to lobby the effort.

Geological ventures were of keen interest because of the rapid expansion of acquired territory under President Polk's administration. States and territories wanted to pinpoint valued resources for the economic growth. Polk's aggressive foreign policies netted so much land in the southwest and northwest that it rivaled President Thomas Jefferson's deal on the Louisiana Purchase. The result eventually ended in the formation of the states of Oregon, Washington, Idaho, California, New Mexico, Arizona, Nevada, Utah and parts of Colorado, Montana, and Wyoming. Mapping and surveying geological features and mineral resources were of keen interest for government and investors (Riccards, 1997.)

In February as Morris solicited subscriptions, he appeared before the Mississippi legislature to encourage the creation of a state geological survey. Morris stated that during this time he "lectured upon the same and kindred (geological) themes while engaged in the business of my agency, before the principal schools of Mississippi and elsewhere" (Rule, 1922, p. 228.) With the influence of friends such as Burney, who had been recently appointed head of the Department of Metaphysics at the University of Mississippi, Morris saw scientific pursuits deeply connected with freemasonry, a fraternal organization that combined concrete elements of nature to symbolize human connections with earth's origin and connection with God. Morris continued his interest of connecting metaphysical symbols with Masonic order and interpretation. These connections are found through his later

Morris's Geology Book "Sparks from a Geologist's Hammer."

Morris attended many legislative sessions at the old State
Capitol (pictured) in Jackson which is now a museum.

years in the Conservator Movement, his published almanacs, and in his hobby of numismatics (study of coins). Morris published his own a numismatic journal from his home after the family's final move to LaGrange, Ky.

Spring 1848 Correspondence and Diary entries from Rob to Charlotte:

Mount Sylvan, Sunday, January 2, 1848

My much loved wife

I have been away from home since last Tuesday. I went to Mr. Frazers on Wednesday. On Thursday it rained all day and so I staid at Frazers. On Friday I went to Major Brahans. On yesterday I came home and today I am at Brother McKays where I was last Sunday when I wrote to you last.

William Brooks took all our things I believe the covers to the skillets were all so broken up that I did not think it worth while to send one. You can buy one in Memphis. I hope every thing arrived safely but it rained so hard on the wagon that I am afraid things got wet. I shall go to Oxford tomorrow and on Tuesday start for Jackson. I feel that I am ready now for business and I want to be out at work. Everything seems to be favorable and I shall be much mistaken if I don't go into good business at once.

Everything looks natural about here. Trigg is getting on very well with this building operations. Bro. Burney is putting up new houses. William Brown is sick. Col. Brown started for Jackson last Tuesday there is quite a number of scholars engaged from all quarters.

I sent you a large letter by Brooks which I hope you got.

There now I have told you all the news.

I have been in dull spirits all last week. The bad weather and my having nothing to do and no books to read or paper to write on made it very unpleasant. I wish I had staid with you a week longer.

Do you think of me Charlotte? Do you pray for me with that love which alone can make a prayer affectual? Remember me often before God and I will remember you.

Show John this letter and get him accustomed to my handwriting so that he will know it. Tell him to be a good boy so Pa will love him and God will love him too. Kiss my sweet little Charlotte for me. The first time that baby Alfred laughs kiss him for Pa.

My heart is with you all

Goodbye from your dear husband. R. Morris

Monday morning, January 17, 1848

I am just starting out to my days work. Have got to call on everybody to get them to come and hear me speak tonight. But I will fill this sheet before I start.

I am suffering this morning from the toothache. It is a cloudy, rainy day and things look a little gloom. I am a little reared at the idea of appearing before so many folks but I have got my speech well by heart and I shall try to do my best. The advantage of all this is it will make me acquainted with the principal men in Mississippi at once. It will give me an acquaintance in every town and village in the state and in my business arrangements it will be greatly in my favor to find folks who know me. Your letter has not come yet and I am afraid it will be too late for me. The mails are monstrous irregular this winter. But I still hope to hear from you and now I will go to work.

Love R.M.

Tuesday Jan. 18, 1848

I got through safely last night had a good audience and was enabled to make a good work of it. But such a dreadful night as I suffered after it from toothache pains me to think of. I have been all the morning at the Dentists who has pulled two teeth, plugged one and filed several more.

Wednesday Jan 19

I got a good nights sleep last night but am most as bad this morning as ever. After bearing it as long as I could I went to the Dentist and had another big tooth pulled so I am easy again. My health is very good and prospects for business excellent. Robert Mckay came here yesterday from Vicksburg. He will ride with me all the winter.

I shall start to Vicksburg tomorrow evening to be gone about a week. When I get back I will write to you. Once more good bye

Your husband R Morris

Canton Mississippi, January, 28 1848,
Addressed as: Samuel Mendenall for Mrs. C. M. Morris, Memphis, Tennessee

My sweet wife and dearly loved Charlotte,

I have got about ten days behind in my letter to you so I will now try to make it up.

Tuesday, January 18

I spent the day groaning with a toothache. I had two pulled but that night the pain was a bad as ever.

Wednesday, January 19

I had another tooth pulled and got well.

Thursday, January 20

I went to Vicksburg on the railroad cars. The distance is about 40 miles and they go in 3 hours. The price is $3.00. My horse was quite sick and I did not feel willing to ride her.

Friday, January 21

I came back to Jackson. My horse was getting well.

Saturday, January 22

I rode to Clinton about 10 miles where I found some very kind friends in the family of Rev. S. Colton, President of the Mississippi College.

Sunday, January 23

Heard two good sermons from Dr. Chamberlain and Mr. Hazzard.

Monday, January 24

Spent the day at Clinton and the night at Mr. MacRowens.

Tuesday, January 25

It rained so hard all day that I staid in the house and went back to Mr. Colton's to spend the night.

Wednesday, January 26

Went to Jackson in the morning found Robert McKay there waiting for me and we came out 10 miles on the Canton road.

Thursday, January 27

Came to Madisonville 10 miles and spent the night with Brother McKee.

Friday, January 28

Went to Canton 8 miles, spent the day there and then out 4 miles to Rev. Mr. Ross a minister in our church. His wife and sister are very kind to us and next to being at home I feel most satisfied when I am at such a place as this.

Saturday, January 29

I came 8 miles to the house of Bro. Muse near Sharon.

Sunday, January 30

I delivered a Sunday school address in Sharon then went to the Methodist meeting and preached in the Cumberland Church at night. Spent the night with Rev. Mr. Adair, a Cumberland preacher.

Monday, January 31

Went to Canton and back with Bro. Muse in his buggy. I wrote a letter to you yesterday and put it in the post office at Canton. It contained $10 for you and I will send you some more very soon. You must be as saving as you can but not stingy. I don't want my wife to be stingy but buy whatever you really need. Keep our dear children neat and clean. Don't' let their clothes get ragged for if they get into dirty habits while they are young they will not easily get over it. I shall be able to keep you in what money you need, if my health continues to be as good as it is at present and when spring opens and the weather gets good I hope to do still better. You know I promised you a negro girl at Christmas or I will buy you a little home of your own just which your please.

This is the finest country I have been in Mississippi. The land is level and rich and dwelling houses are most all frame houses, the people are wealthy and sociable and the climate appears very healthy.

I was asked to deliver another lecture in Jackson before I left but I could not stay any longer Col. Brown seems to be very much thought of there. He told me that he had just got a letter from Mrs. Porter stating that her brother in law, Mr. Caruthers was lately scalded to death on a steamboat. That was a dreadful death indeed. I saw him at Col. Browns last year.

Can my little baby Alfred crawl any yet? Does the sweet Charlotte whine any of nights? Does John beat his drum any or has he worn it all out?

And do you , dear, wife, think often of your husband who thinks so often of you. Do you pray for me and wish that my soul may be preserved form evil and that I may be brought safely back to your arms.

May the Savior of souls keep you all
From yours, R. Morris

Read all my letters to John and let him be glad to have the time come when he shall learn to write to me. There are a great many children here old and young and one of the boys keeps asking me questions about my pencil and my letter and everything else just as John used to.

I got a chance to day to see the *Banner of Peace* for the first time since I left home. Once more goodbye.

Near Kosciusk, Altal County, Mississippi
February 3, 1848

My Dear Wife

I find that in this business I need a great many different agencies. Some folks want one kind of newspaper and some another. Some want Democrat and some Whig, some scientific, some literary, some religious. Among them all I get a good many subscribers and when I get the rest of my agencies I shall do still better.

The little trunk is not very much in the way only it keeps me from reading on the horseback as I need both hands to hold on by. I think I will have a pair of saddlebags fixed against my next trip and not take the trunk.

Greensboro, Choctaw County, Mississippi
February 10, 1848

I started Robert McKay this morning to Mount Sylvan. He is to meet me on Friday, February 18 at Black hawk—is a town about 40 miles from this place. My object in sending him is to get some more samples. To get what letters maybe in the post office and to hear from you. I wrote to Hunt to let me know if he had heard from any of you since I left for I am getting very anxious, my wife, to hear from you.

Robert has been good company to me and is indeed a faithful fellow. He reads his testament four chapters a day, writes home twice a week to his parents and keeps a diary of all that happens to us in our journey .I hope we shall be able to raise our boys Alfred and John and all the others which we may have, to be as good and religious as he is.

This county is very muddy now and Fanny finds it hard work to get along but she keeps up her spirits and is always gay and merry when we start in the morning. Tell Brother John that Fanny can jump further than he can, and when she sees me coming she nickers after me and tries to break her bridle to get at me.

Van Buren April 6, 1848

My Dear Charlotte

I am waterbound here and it is raining hard so I don't know when I can get away. I wrote to you last Saturday in Fulton. On Sunday April 2 I delivered a Sabbath School's Address in Fulton. I staid there till Tuesday and then came 10 miles to this place. In crossing the Bigbee river I met with an accident. The water is out in the bottom and I had to wade a quarter of a mile. In going through a treetop Fanny got scared, jumped hard, broke the girth round her breast, the saddle slipped back, scared her still worse, the other girth broke and I was thrown off into the water with saddle and everything. The water was about three feet deep. I picked up my things and laid them on logs, then went on to the ferry boat. It was deep and hard wading.

When I got to the river, I called till I was hoarse and no one came. It was sunset, Fanny was gone, I was chilled and tired and don't think I could have lived to wade a quarter of a mile back. But the Ferryman came, we found Fanny, rode back and gathered up my things, crossed the river and the man made me stay with him. He gave me dry clothes, took out all my clothes and papers and dried them, and the next morning I felt as well as ever. These kind people were named Priddy, they would not take a cent for anything they did. You must remember their goodness to your husband.

Last night I gave these people an Address and today I am just doing nothing but reading. I have some good news to tell you. I am now thinking it likely I will go to General Assembly which meets in Memphis, about the 20th May. You can see the time in the Banner. This will bring us together two or three weeks sooner that we expected but I will be able to tell you more correctly in a few days.

I hope you have not had any sickness among the children since

I left. I often think of your hard watching and sitting up with poor little Alfred last winter. That was worthy of a mother's love and will be rewarded no doubt by his growing up a stout healthy man.

I know that it is putting too much on you to make you bear all the trouble of raising our children but I shall try to be with you as much as I can and after a while shall expect to settle myself again.

Show John and Charlotte my name and talk to them about Pa, if they love him or want to see him.

Read over the letter I wrote you about Christmas and try to act it out.

Don't forget me day or night,

Your husband R. Morris

Van Buren, Mississippi, April 8, 1848 (excerpt of letter)

My Dear Wife

I wrote a letter yesterday from this place and you will get them both at the same time but I don't believe you would be sorry to get four or five.

I am still waterbound and it is raining hard. I have not been much lonesome but if your company or even one of the babies to play with I could do better a good deal. I have been thinking today how I wish we had a little home of our own like that one in DeSoto, with garden and cornfield and houses enough and old Betsey. I am sure you will agree with me in the wish and do all you can to labor and save that we may get such a home again.

Indeed you have always been disposed to save all you could and I am satisfied that you will do it yet. Our chance is certainly good now to have more property by this time next year than we had in DeSoto and if I can get my health I shall not cease to make every effort to secure us a home.

Pray for me dear Charlotte, that I may succeed in my undertaking and be kept pure from the vices and evils of life. Since I left home I have subscribers to the amount of one hundred and seventy dollars. Out of this there is a profit of more than fifty dollars. This is doing pretty well.

But my poor little black Testament was wet through and through when I was thrown in the water and the cover is coming off, I am staying with Bro. Harbour, they are excellent people, have no

State chambers of the Old State Capitol in Mississippi where Morris
made several appeals to establish a state geological division.

Charlotte Mendenall Morris in her early thirties.
Courtesy of The Grand Chapter of Kentucky, OES.

children but as friendly as friends can be.

I find my flute great company such a day as this, people get tired of talking and I get tired of reading and then for a little music, to enliven us all up.

I wrote today to Bro. Cosset that I would probably meet him in Memphis at the General Assembly and if I do you may look for me something sooner than we expected to meet.

It maybe however that Assembly meets in June if so there will be no alteration but I shall be with you between the seventh or tenth of June.

I have found out that I can frank letters while I am traveling this saves me some postage and will enable me to write oftener than I should have done.

My dear wife goodbye. I would put my arms round you and draw you to my heart if I could and then I would whisper good bye.

Heaven smiles be with you.

Your affectionate husband R. Morris

Aberdeen April 17 1848

My Dear Charlotte

I meant to write a long letter to you on yesterday but we had so much company I could not find time.

I dated my last letter April 8. The next day I preached in Van Buren.

On April 10 I went to Richmond 8 miles and gave a Sunday school address. On April 12 I went about 12 miles, was stopped by a creek so I staid with Mr. Trice. April 12 I went 10 miles to Okolona and gave an address. April 14 I came here 20 miles and have been here ever since. I preached yesterday from this last verse of Romans 6 Chapter. I stay with Bro. Porter ,an excellent man.

The General Assembly meets in Memphis May 16 and I shall be there if nothing happens, only four weeks more. God bless my dear children

From your husband R. Morris

The following are Charlotte's letters and diary entries to Rob during the spring of 1848.

January 12,1848

Shelby County, Tennessee

My Dear husband

This is the first opportunity that I have had to rite to you. Sinc you left here sis took sick on Thursday after you left and Alfred on Friday night and john on Saturday night. The doctor attended to John and Alfred. John had the winter fever and Alfred had the aviccus.They are all getting well but it has bin a trying sene to all in both body and mind and I wept over them night and day and no one to shear the load of sorrow but me and me along. But god was with me, he new all my sorrow I prayed most earnestly unto him and I feel he heard my prayers.

We moved home new years day—our things got here the day before but the rocking chair it got one leg tore out and the nigger made me pay twenty five sents for bringing over it. I am writing to you to nigh with my sick boy in my lap because I feel as if I had not done my duty to you. But I think you cannot complain. You wrote to commence with John on new years day but I will be gin with him as he gets stout enough.

I think the first of March all most like in age.But I wont let my self think over it no more than I can help. If I must it would greve me so much that I cold not stand it. But I think all the time about the present hours that we will spend together when you come home and pray god that we may see them happy hours.

Well my little boy is getting restless and my light is giving out so must say good bye. May god be with you now and forever.

Yours most truly

Charlotte Morris

Charlotte's Diary Entries January-February 1848

Jan 15th

My dear husband we are all well at this time and to day I am alone and I fell as if never would see you again.

Jan 16th

Today is Sunday and it is a verry rany day. John and sis has gone to gran pa and there is narry baby with me but Pony (nickname for Alfred).

Jan 17

Today I went to fathers and I brought john home and left sis there and I have had john reciting his lesson to day. But I think he is a hard case

Jan 18

The childrens all well to day and john says that pa has gone to get monny and when he comes home he can by his floot.

Jan 19

To day Wilson has gone to Memphis and I expect two or three letters from you

Jan 20

I got three letter from you last night the first one that I red was from Mount Sylvan the seond was from carelton the third was from rev. Andrew Herons Holmes County. It gave great pleasure to read it. I red it over and over. I commenced with John the 19th day of January and to day I have had him saying his lesson. I told him that pa sayd if he would learn to before he come home he would by him a floot. I have commenced reding the Bible again. I have neglected it on the count of sick children. But I hope I wont have it to do again. You asked me if I ever thought of you. I do it is the last thing of night and the first thing of a morning and I allways pray for you.

Jan 21

Today I am here nursing Pony. It takes a bout all of my time to nurse and cook and do my writing and and reading and hear John's lessons. Little sis come home today and I told her what paw sayed and she sayed did he. the childrens all well today and I thank god for it.

Jan 22

This is Saturday night and I feel verry low spirited and tierd for I have been washing today. This is the 22 day of January and but wish it was the 15th of March. I think all over some times and I think it verry hard that them that ought to be together has to be so far apart. It sems to me some times that I cannot stand it to see Wilson making uncle of his little Boy and little Alfred looking on as much as to say that I haven't got any paw here to call me a swet boy. It brings tears from my eyes. But I trust in my god that he will have paw here by the 15th of March. If I could express my feelings to wards you I could tell you a great deal with this but must say farewell. But still remains your true love.

Charlotte Morris

Jan. 2
Shelby County, Tennessee

My most Dear Robert, I am going to fathers to day but I must do my duty first. I feel sick to day. But I will go rather than to stay by myself. The childrens all well to day and very hapy at the thought of going to gran pars

Jan 24

I have had company to day and have been very busy. So I took your time for riting by candle ligt I can think better what I want to rite about. So when I am done my riting I have my chapter in the Bible to read. I wish I had you here when I red the Bible to explain the words that I don't understand. I think it would be all most the greatest pleasure in the world. Jon has ben saying his lesson to day as usual but I am feared he wont learn he don't care anything at all about his Book

Jan 25

It is raining to day and I feel all most out of hart wailing for the first of march. It seems like an age. I am reading Hester an rogers now and my Bible. I wish I new whare you was to night. John ask me to say whare was paw and he wished he new whare paw was. He wanted to see him mity bad and little sis was standing by and she sayed that paw was gone home. Brooks has gone to day after his second wife. He is to be mared to night to Miss allen.

Jan 26

To day is wet with thunder. I have got the toothache and my patience wont let me rite much but I will try. I am doing my duty to day reading and riting and hearing Johns lesson. Little sis keep me up all night last night. She was sick with the colry morbus but she appears to be well today. John and Alfred is both well.

Jan 28

I have bin washing to day and my fingers is very stiff and so you must excuse the riting. The old lady Brooks has bin here a visiting to day. But I was washing so I wasn't in her company much. The childrens all well to day little Alfred has two teeth and I do assure you that he can bite some.

Jan 27

This is the twenty ninth of January and I feel tonight that I could not wait for the 15th of march. Come home and see me do my own cooking and washing. It appears like old times to me if at last was you here. I wish you new how much I loved you and how I feel to wards you to night. My heart feels over loaded while I am trying to tell you about it and I cant help wondering to my self is you ever would read this. John says he loves paw but he has to go and get monny. He will come home after a while and little sis says tell paw that she loves him and Alfred still says paw paw but he don't now that he has a paw in this world and don't care is to get plenty to eat and maw to amuse him. We are all well to day the lord has ben with us and he has promised be with us to the end . with this say good night. But still remain your true love. Charlotte Morris

Jan 31 1848

My most beloved husband

Today is Sunday and the last day of January and I received two letters from you to day which I broke open with great ansiety. And when I read them I was glad to that your health was good but that you had three teeth pulled out and severl pluged and I am afeard that it is your riding in the cold and I feel uneasy about it for I fear it will make you sick. But I hope that god will protect you from all danger. I told John and Sis that they must not for get to love paw and John says he loved paw mity good and sis says do you John I do two. We are all well to day and hope that you are

Feb 1 1848

I stayed at fathers last night and got home agin to do my duty. Mother came home with me for the first visit she has stayed us. I left John and Sis with grand paw. I feel very loan some when they are both gone.

Feb 2

To day Sarah stayed with us today. Old Mr. Kil Patrick come here to after mr. Wilson to finish his house and I expect he will do so and myself and I am will be left alone but it only makes me feel gloomy to see them together but I hope it is god will to be with them. I love my loving husband the time has bin swet and we spend with you.

> My swet and harmless dove
> Thus for my god has led me on
> And made his truth and mercy known
> My hopes and fears alternate rise
> And comforts mingle with my signs

Feb 3

It is very wet and cold. But I feel intolerable good spirits the time will soon come that me and my dear Robert will be together again. We are all well to day

Feb 4

To day is verry cold windy day and the fire we all around us. John and sis is at grand paws. John is not learning any thing and it is await on my mind. The house has smoked all and my eyes feels like their all most out.

Feb 5

It is cold to day. John and sis is still at grand paws they have bin thare nearly all week and I feel anxious to see them. John sayed paw stays so long he wonders if he will even see paw any more. I told him that God would take care of paw and bring back again. I have tried to do every thing you avised me to but John I can't get him to learn any thing at all about his book and i don no what to do about it. I feel uneasy about it for I no you will expect me to do a gret deal in the way of educating him. Everything else I have don. I am reading my bible and sayin my prarers and loving you for you are my dayly thoughts. it is all I live for to love you and for you . if I had you here to night I would be as happy as I came to be—don't wait for the 15th of march. We are all well to night and pray god you with this good night I still remain your true love
Charlotte morris

Feb. 14

The house caught a fire last night and burnt the fire place so bad that we cant have nay fire

Feb 15

Today I have to leave home on the account of the chimney they are bilding a new one.

Feb 27

Today I have bin coocking in the old smoky kitchin and my eyes is nearly smoked out. John still says his lesson every day. I find no trobel at all to get him to say his lessons. Sis is still at granpaws and pony (Alfred) is still creeping over the floor and all I lack of being happy to night my be loved Robert is not here with us. The childrens all well to night.

Rob returned home during March and then left during April and most of May. The following are diary entries from Charlotte while living at Shelby County Tennessee in April 1848.

April 9

My Kind Husband: this is the 9th letter I have commence to you and it is lik you was with me all the time. I stayed at Uncle Isaac last night and today I am at Father's. The children's is all well but little Bob is sich yet.

The 10th

I am at home again and Mother come home with me and spent the day. Our children is all well yet but Robert Wilson is verry sick, the dr. was with him to night and he told us that Uncle Isaac had the mumps and he thought it was very awful case with him.

The 11th

I have bin sick to day. I sit up last night . sit up all night and all the work to do and sick at that. It makes me feel like some old wore out Negro. But I hope it with tolerable good patience the children is all well to night. Oh where are you tonight. I would give all the world to see you to night. Uncle Isaac is quite sick yet.

April 12

I have bin cooking and nursing all day and I feel all most wore out and expect to sit all night. Robert Wilson is quite sick and I think that whether he lives or not I think it doubtful. My self our childrens all well to my self I am not but I recon it is only fatigue. I pray God to spare our little ones . Where is my love to night. Will we see him again. I hope that God's mercy will bring him back to me again. I hope that God's mercy will bring him back to me again by the 10th of June. The 10th of June is my only thoughts.

April 13th

I have bin lying down and I feel quite sick to night. The children's all well to night.

The 14th

I am sick yet and my arms aches so bad that I can scarsley hold the pen at all. But I received your letter to day. Makes me feel a great deal better . There is but nothing in the world that pleases me than to get a letter from you and that is to have you with me that is worth all the world besides our childrens all well to night.

My dear Robert and kind Husband I am at Uncle Isaacs to day and it is Sunday and my thoughts is intirely for you the more I am in Company the more I think of you I feel uneasy for something will happen to you so I will not see you any more and oh what a time that would be to me our children as all well

The 17th

I am at home again and I feel quite low spirited to night I look round and I don't see my kind husband smiling on Me oh it makes me feel so gloomy But when I am done my Riting I will read my Bible and I think it will rouse me up some our Babes is well and as swet as ever

The 18th

I have been making soap today and the wind has blew hard all day and it is getin quite cold the wind never blows but I think of you my rober and it never tuns cold for the rain never falls but I think of you whare you are whether you are comfortable or if your out in the cold but I no god takes care of us all the children all well to night the 19th

I am verry tired to night for I have bin making soap and that is very tire some but since and the times is getting quite hard here for us for we have sat the last pease of meal that there is in the smoke house and worse that there is no money and I call that close by hard time but our babies is well and that is enough

the 20th

I have bin a washing to day and I feel quite low spirited to night it is so long tell the 10 of June But if it a good while I hope it will be the pleasenter when It comes but seem to me that I canot wait that long John still says his lessons ever day but I have hime to whip some times we are all well to night have you and do you feel as anxious about me as I do about you

the 21st

I have just finished my ironing and have sit down to my writing every body is gone to bed and is a sleep and so I am alone every thing looks dark and gloomy John is crying with the tooth ache to night sis and Alfred is well

April 22 1848

I have bin busy all day and all the time wishing for night to come for they have gone to Germantown and I expect to get a letter from you that is next best to me in the world the children is all well and John and Sis has gone a visiting this evening to gran pa

My dear Beloved Husband

They have got home from German town and I got two letters from you rit in at van Buren. One I red with tears in my eyes whare you was in the wqter and when you went back to the ferry and could not make any one hear for some time what would you have done if you could not have made them heard you at all you must have a great deal But to was the last part of suffered it was much more pleasant for you sayed more than likely you would be a home by the 20th of May that was v erry pleasant news in deed to Me so good night my dear Robert and kind husband your true wife

Charlotte Morris

April the 23rd 1848

My Dear Robert and Husband coming home I am in good spirits to day on the thought of you I cant keep from talking about it for am all the time a think about it I am refered it is two good news to be true But hope so John has had the tooth ache now three days

April 24th

I did not sleep my last night for John was havin distracted with the tooth ache I don't o what to do with him for he has had it now four days and his face is sweld up so he don't look like himself Sis and Alfred is well to night

the 25th

John is still criing with the tooth aches and I am aferd it is ago-ing to rise poor little Boy he is suffering a great deal I don't know what to do I cant bear the idea of having it puld if Pa was hereand tell a poor ignorant woman what to do it is bad for one to live and feel as if they war distitute of friends when our children gets sick no kind friend to go to But I put my trust in god for I no he is a friend to all who love and obay for there is no respect of persons with god

the 26th

I have bin busy all day trying to makeing me a new dress But it is verry cold and it keep me nearly all the time to keep the Children warm for I have to pack the wood from the woods John is better with the tooth ache But he is aresting badly to night I feel verry uneasy a bout him oh come home and shear with me a trobel mind about sick children where are you to night are in a warm house I do pray that you were not in the wet and cold but I hope you are with kind friends and will have warm bed to sleep in

the 27th

I have bin washing to day and I feel verry tired to Night But as tired as i am I don't for get My Dear beloved Husband that is far away from Me and I am always thinking about him and my most earnest prarers is for him and My heart yearns for him I don't think I can stand this way of living what is the world to Me and all I live for and all I care for so far away from me My body is here But My thoughts is with you every minute and every hour and every day and every week and every Month John is nearly well of the tooth ache sis and Alfred is well

the 28th

this day five years ago mr little Robert died and oh what an awful time that was But how he is now with his god Ready to receive his father and mother and brother and sister I do Most earnestly pray that all our Children will be happy when they die as he now I the children is all well once More

the 29th

Elish and Mary come here last Night and they have gone to father today and I am going this evening their coming only serves to make me gloomy I cant cant enjoy my self any a tall here for I don't know where you are sick or not or you may be dead and me not no it the children is all well John asks every day How long will it Be Before Pa come home and sis says does Pay wants to see his bad cat mity bad

the 30th

I am at fathers to day I am here with my friends But I feel as if My friend is not here where is he I no not But I hope that he is with a kind friend with this I say god bless you
Yours truly Charlotte Morris

CHAPTER FOUR

A Pivotal Time for the Morris Family

On Feb. 7, 1848, the Mississippi State Legislature incorporated the Trustees of the Eureka Masonic College at Richland, Holmes County giving the Trustees of the Eureka Masonic College the "power to confer literary and honorary degrees." The college had formerly been established as the Richland Literary Institute when its cornerstone was dedicated in 1847 (*The Freeman's Monthly*, 1848.) The trustees of the college were to have at "least the Third Degree of Masonry" and be associated with the Eureka Lodge No. 61, Lexington Lodge No. 24 and the Lexington Royal Arch Chapter. In addition, the legislation stated that the Grand Lodge of Mississippi shall take the Masonic College "under its patronage."

During his travels through Mississippi, Morris associated with Eureka Lodge No. 61 at Black Hawk and received his Royal Arch Degree from the Lexington Royal Arch Chapter through the affiliation at Eureka Lodge (which was later renamed Moriah Lodge.) Lodge records from the Lexington Royal Arch Chapter in 1848 indicated that Morris taught at Eureka Masonic College during the summer of 1848. As Rob became acquainted with a new prospect of activities at the Eureka Masonic College near Black Hawk, Mississippi, he became interested in moving Charlotte and the children from Germantown, Tennessee to Black Hawk to live.

Author's note: Today the Eureka Masonic College is a historic site known as The Little Red Schoolhouse . It is owned and managed by the Order of the Eastern Star in Mississippi and a tourist attraction (National Register of Historic Places, 1970.)

The first mention of Black Hawk by Morris came from the following letter written to Charlotte in June:

Black Hawk June 4, 1848

My dear wife

I devote this Sunday morning to you. I got to Mount Sylvan on Saturday night after I left you and preached there the next day to a good audience. All is well about our old home and many inquiries were made about you. I called a Colonel Brown, McKay, Burney, spending one night with Joshua and one with hunt. Hunt had got a horse and will start out on our Agency this week. He thinks he will do well. They have the hopping cough about that neighborhood but none had died.

On Monday I left and got here on Wednesday, ever since I came I have been writing day and night, am through now and shall leave here on Tuesday but don't know yet which way I will go.

Our business has gone on well and we all feel encouraged. We are very warmly invited to live here and I think we shall do well to come down in the Fall. Yesterday I preached in the Baptist Church and in the evening delivered an address at the laying of the corner-stone of a new Masonic Hall which has just been commenced here. I got a letter from my sister who says there is no news yet, all well.

And now my thoughts rant to that dear family of which you are the mother and I think I see you and hear you all and I hear my sweet children asking about me and wishing that I would come home to see them again. I will write to them a little letter.

My dear boy

I want my son to be a good boy all the time, to love his dear sister, to mind what ma tells him, to be kind to the dear baby and never to tell a lie. I wrote a little verse that I want you to learn before I come home. Here it is:

> I 'm nothing but a little boy
> My name is brother John sir,
> But I can spell and read it well
> And whistle when I'm done sir
> I'll never fight my little sis
> I'll never tell a lie sire
> I'll play with pony when he wakes
> And nurse him if he cry sir.

If my dear boy will learn this little verse will Pay will love him dearly.

My dear little daughter

Pa's daughter must be a good girl and when Pa comes home you may climb up on the bed with me and lay on my arm.

Whatever you have to do always find time for Johns lesson and get him so that he can spell before I come back

If you ever get tired and discouraged read Isaiah, forty first chapter; tenth verse and you will find such precious promises that

The Eureka Masonic College (pictured) known as The Little Red Schoolhouse, is a historic site and museum dedicated to Rob Morris, operated by The Grand Chapter of Mississippi, OES.

Darlene Roberts and Claude Carnathan hold Minutes book, Royal Arch Chapter, Nov. 9, 1848, requiring charges to the Eureka Masonic College for fees rendered by Rob Morris.

Minutes from the Royal Arch Chapter book, Nov. 9, 1848 that showed payment owed to Rob Morris for his work at Eureka College. *Courtesy of the Grand Chapter of Mississippi, OES.*

you cannot help being satisfied with them

I am pleased to remember how much your are improved in your patience and good temper. There is a great alteration in you but don't stop at that but keep on improving until you have a perfect command of yourself and never get out of patience again. Every time you give way to bad felling it will weaken your influence with your children and make you less useful. I am trying hard to overcome my pride and impatience and hope, under God, to succeed until I gain a perfect victory.

And now I commend you all to him who raised the Lord Jesus from the dead and offers salvation to all who believe in his name. I should be glad to spend this Sunday with you but as I cannot I will send you my love and my prayers from your husband

R. Morris

Keep baby Alfred carefully!

During this month, Charlotte writes to inform Rob that whopping cough has taken the children ill:

June the 14th

Mr Dear Husband

This is the first tie that I have tempted to rite any sense you left home I looked for your home a the end of two weeks but now it is nearly three and I have given it up in dipar I haven't herd word from you since you left I do feel so much disappointed I do feel so gloomy to Night a wandering husband and three sick children at home they have all got the hoppin cough little sis is getting better but John and Alfred is quit sick yet I feel verry uneasy about them and more anxious to have their kind farther with them

June 15th

We are left all alone and it is a gloomy time Wilson left home to day for kilpatricks and wont be at home any more in three weks and I told him not to come back here any more until you come for I don't like to see them ? for it only makes me feel like some one that was deserted the children aint any better yet

June the 16th

Today Mother come and spent the day with us and I think the

Childrens some better to night

June the 17th

   Have Bin washing to day but I can't as much at it for the Children is all sick.

In June 1848, Morris left Black Hawk to make an extended tour through the northern and eastern states including a visit to see his siblings. This was the first time Morris had seen his siblings since he had left Massachusetts at age 18 and ventured west.

He visited Masonic lodges and collected Masonic literature. He observed that there were quite a number of different ways that Masonic lodges operated and was disturbed at the lack of uniformity on rituals and governance. Uniformity and governance was characteristic of the Whig Party of which Morris was a supporter. General Zachary Taylor was the Whig Party candidate for president in 1848 and Morris contributed articles for the *Whig Party Flag*. On a steamboat trip Morris mentioned passing the home of William Henry Harrison, a Whig Party president who died in office a few days after his inauguration. In later correspondence Morris talked about his admiration for Henry Clay, a mason and very powerful Whig Party member, who at one time had been Grand Master of the Grand Lodge of Kentucky (Riccards, 1997.)

The Whigs celebrated Clay's vision of the American System that promoted rapid economic and industrial growth in the United States. Government should support modern, market-oriented economy where expertise and bank credit would count for more than physical strength or land ownership. Infrastructure such as canals and railroads needed to expand. Public school systems, private colleges, charities and cultural institutions were an important part of the party's platform (Ibid.) All of these elements closely aligned with Morris's ideals.

The following two letters that he sent to Charlotte focused on his steamboat trip and visit to Washington from June 27–July 20, 1848.

   Another bad night's rest- the floors are hard beds with only our blanket to lie on but I shall get used to them I suppose.
   The gambling still goes on and one man has lost all his money.
   After sundown we passed Madison and soon after that I went to sleep. When I got up I found we had just passed north Bend where

General Harrison lived. At 9 o'clock we arrived at Cincinnati. After I got this far the Captain told me he should not start today so I put on clean clothes and went to meeting. First I went to a church where they talk Dutch. They sing and pray and preach all in Dutch. I could not understand it so I went to a Presbyterian Church and took the sacrament with them. At night I went to hear Mr. Rice, the same man who had the debate with Campbell. I have got the book at home.

He preached an excellent sermon. Then I came back to the boat and slept as well as the muschitoes would let me.

July 3

Right on the other side of the river is a company of soldiers drilling. Tell John they look mighty pretty with their guns and all dressed alike. They right face and left face and march and halt just as we used to at Mount Sylvan.

I wrote a letter to Joshua Brown and some others telling them how well I love to think of Mount Sylvan and the happy days we enjoyed there.

We left Cincinnati about noon having been detained more than five days which I don't like a bit but I can't help it and it is best to be patient. I hope now that we shall get along pretty fast.

We can get to Maysville about 9 o'clock and soon after that I want to slepp

July 4

Last night was so cold that I feel a little unwell this morning. I cant pull the bedclothes over me or creep up close to you when I get cold, as I used to do at home, all I can do is shiver a little and go to sleep again

A little child of the Captain's died last night on the boat. It was a sickly infant four months old and never had been well but I cannot help thinking of our grief when our sweet Robert died and how we would have given all the world to save his precious life so I feel for this father and mother who loved the little baby that now lies dead in the cabin.

This is the Fourth of July but I have seen but few signs of it. In Portsmouth I noticed a few soldiers in handsome uniform but no cannon nor music.

The fellow that took my medicine has improved so much that

he looks like another man and he thinks I must be quite a doctor.

It is good to see what an improvement there is already among these rough men in the way of swearing. Very few of them will swear before me now although I have only been on the boat five days and when I first came on board you could hear it all the time. The worst swearer in the whole promised he would quit if I would write a letter for him to one of his friends because he can't write and he is trying right hard to keep his promise.

One of the passengers is going on shore at Greenupsburg and promises to put this letter in the office so I must close it up. Good bye my dear Partner in life. Think of me and remember me before all others except god.

From your loving friend

R. Morris

July 5 4 o'clock p.m.

My Dear Wife

I sent a letter to you yesterday of two sheets As I begin to draw nearer to Baltimore my time will be more occupied and my chance to write you long letters will not be good so I had better begin to day.

I expect to get to Wheeling tomorrow noon and there take the stage so if I do I can probably get to Baltimore by Saturday night and I can go in two hours to Washington. It is likely that Congress may break up Saturday night and then I don't know that I shall go to Washington at all.

I caught a bad cold and a sore throat last night and fell a little unwell in consequences. The river is getting more narrower up there than it was.

The next time I go to New York I must take John with me for company and you may tell him so if he is a good boy. He would make this long journey much pleasanter with his talk and it will be a good plan to let him see something of the world as young as possible.

July 6th

We got to Wheeling by nine o'clock this morning but there is not stage going out before 6 o'clock tomorrow morning. This keeps me here a whole day and as I have nothing on earth to do it makes me a great deal more fretful than a good Christian might to be. This is quite a large city. I was here in 1839 and took the same road that I am to take tomorrow. This is the same house that I ate a Christmas dinner in when old Felix Grundy was here with me.

I was then a young man and he an old one. He is dead and I am here with nine years more on my head and my heart with my little wife and three children far off in Tennessee.

What a change does nine years make. I am going to meet those who have not all three been together for 15 years and then I shall part with them expecting to meet them nor more this side of death. May God grant that all of us may meet in heaven where we shall not part again and there I want you and Little John and sweet Charlotte and baby Alfred and dead little Robert to help me make up a family circle in this kingdom of glory. Oh this will be what we shall gain by Jesus' love to us

My fare to Philadelphia is thirteen dollars but then I shall be within 8 hours of New York and about 12 more of my brother and sister. I have written to John to come part way and meet me if he possibly can and I think he will.

I sent a letter today to the *Banner of Peace* which will be printed and I want you to read it to see how I spent last Sunday. It is called "A Sabbath in Cincinnati by a Cumberland Minister" and you will get it in about four weeks. I have also written a good many letters for a newspaper called The Whig Flag which you will get at Germantown. They are signed M ...

I draw my dear wife close to my bosom and whisper something in her ear. Can she guess what it is?

Farewell from your husband
R. Morris

Washington City, July 9, 1848

My Dear Charlotte:

I had just sealed a letter for you when the stage came for me and hurried me off from Wheeling. We left on Thursday evening at 4'50" o'clock and got to Cumberland and 130 miles and fifty hours by traveling night and day only stopping long enough to eat. It rained most of the time, the stages was full and the weather so cold that if I had not had my blanket, I should have suffered severely. We left Cumberland at 8 o'clock yesterday morning, came 195 miles in ten hours by main road and I got here by 8 o'clock last night, tired enough, you may be sure. I got to bed last night for the first time in two weeks and slept so late this morning they had to keep breakfast for me. I am a little rested now but feel sore and stiff. My appetite is good and I am thankful to have got so near the end of my journey.

I have been to Sunday School this morning and to meetings. Everything to very splendid here but I have not any body yet that I know.

I will write to you again in a few days. I am going to write a little letter to my son John

Washington July 11, 1848

My dearly beloved wife

I sent you a letter two days ago and as these Congress men frank my letters I will write again.

I am now well and busy looking and talking and hearing. I shall leave here Thursday the 13th for Baltimore.

My friends in Mississippi are kind to me and will do all that I ask them to do. Jacob Thompson got back today and is immediately offered me any assistance I wanted. William Brown is expected here this week and I may hear some news from Mount Sylvan.

Good Bless and love you all my sweet wife
Kiss all the babies for me
Your true friend
R. Morris

New York City, July 20, 1848

My Beloved Wife

It is more than a week since I sent you a letter and it has been such a busy week for me that I can hardly think it all over.

On July 13 I left Washington for Baltimore and got there in two hours. I staid there till 6 o'clock in the evening and then by the railroad to Philadelphia. I staid in Philadelphia till Tuesday morning July 18 and then came here in 6 hours.

Our denomination has a church in Philadelphia and I preached there twice on Sunday. They were very kind to me and made my stay there quite a pleasant one. They gave me a call to move there and preach for me offering me a good salary.

It is a fine place and I have no doubt we would do well there.

I start at 5 o'clock this evening and expect to meet my brother and sister tomorrow. My heart will rejoice to see them.

I did not find a letter here from them as I expected which disappointed me.

I have found my old city a good deal as it was when I left it. Everything moves fast. People walk fast and build fast and do business fast and die fast and spend money fast. Every body seem to be in a hurry and by walking so fast on the hard roads I have tired and lamed and blistered my poor feet badly.

I received two letters from Black hawk in Philadelphia by which I learn that all is doing well there.

I have succeeded well in every thing which I came for and have to thank God for all his mercies to me in preserving my health and giving me prosperity in my business.

And now let me ask how does my dear woman get along without me. Does she ever think of the man who has loved her for seven years and hopes to love her till his death.

Does she think often of the father of her children. Does she mingle his name in all her prayers to God and does she hope that in a few more weeks she will embrace him again with joy.

I send my love to the children for I want you to not let them forget me.

Is Johns watermelon ripe yet and has he eat it all up. Is little Charlotte at home or at grandpa's. Has Alfred's cough got well and do his little eyes shine bright again, can he walk any and talk any.

All these questions I want to ask you but I am here far in a distant land and nobody to talk to me as you would talk.

Well goodbye then for a few weeks longer and continue to keep all your affection warm and if it please God to bring me back I will tell you how well I love you.

I am in haste

Farewell your dear husband R. Morris

After returning from his visit to his brother and sister and other areas in the East during July 1848, Morris visited Germantown, Tennessee where his wife and children were living, then returned to Black Hawk by September, selling subscriptions and books around the Black Hawk area. Rob Morris discussed moving the family to Black Hawk and mentioned the Female

Academy (Eureka College.) The following group of letters written by Rob to wife Charlotte, described his activities at Black Hawk.

Black Hawk, September 11, 1848

My Dear Wife

I was sorry to leave you while you were sick but business called me and I could not stay. I got here Saturday night after spending a night with Kelsey, Mr. A. Burney, Mr. A. Bryan and Mr. Gray. All well at Hunt's. She promised to write to you last week. The Mount Sylvan Academy is doing well, about 36 scholars. Major Gray and family seem to be getting on about right. Bro. Cowan was there, he has been sick. I was at camp meeting one night at Rock Spring, not much doing. I saw most of our old neighbors. Yesterday I preached for the Methodists, ten miles from here, from Luke 14, 16.

I now send you ten dollars. Pay your father four dollars of it and do what is best with the rest. The piece of paper in this letter is for Brown Falls and McDavitt of Memphis when you send for that box of books. Get your shells and things out of the box. Then are a good many books which were presents to me. I want you to pick out a sample of each kind of magazine and newspaper in that box and to send it by mail to Mr. W. L Bradley, Senatobia P.O., Desoto Co., MS.

You had better put all in one bundle tie it very tight with strings and paste it. Make up another just such bundle and send to hunt at Mount Sylvan.

I have so much to do today that I must close. My health is good and I hope you have got well.

Yours affectionately, R. Morris

Black Hawk, September 15, 1848

My Dear Wife

I wrote a short letter to you last Monday Sept 11 and sent you ten dollars. I now sit down determined to fill up the whole sheet if I can find anything to say. And certainly I can find words to write when I am writing to my dear wife whom I love better than any body else and to my dear children of whom I think so often.

I have set still this blessed week writing, while my partners are all out of town in business. This is tiresome work and I would much rather be riding than writing. I expect to leave here next Tuesday

Sept. 19 but I don't know yet which way I shall go I am compelled to return back here by the first of October so that I shall not have time to go far. You shall hear from me every week which ever way I travel and I hope it will not be long before we meet.

I was very sorry to leave you sick and would not have done it only I was obliged to. I hope you are now well and that I shall find you looking so when I return.

You have so much work to do that I don't wonder at your having a brush of the chills but if you took the medicine that I gave you I don't doubt it will cure you with God's blessing to go with it.

Poor Brother Bryan has been very low and Mary has such a bad cough I don't see how she can get well. Their camp meeting at Oakland commences today and I am disappointed at not being able to go but I must sit here with this old pen and write till my brains get addled.

I preached last Sunday and have an appointment here for next Sunday in the Baptist Church ... Have a time every day and don't anything but sickness take you form the reading the Bible and secret prayer.

Robert McKay has been a little sick and James Vineyard a good deal. Vineyard will certainly join Presbytery this Fall and became a preacher.

He will probably quit our business. Mr. McKay has been to Arkansas—he was looking at the country and his neighbors think he will move there.

The revival was not at Mount Sylvan but at Black Jack. There were about 25 professors and the whole church seems to be warmer.

I am in good health and spirits. Kiss my dear children. Tell Grundy I shall write before long.

From him who loves you best.

R. Morris

By the Fall of 1848, Rob was satisfied with the Black Hawk community as a new home for his family and looked for a home site for a family move to Black Hawk. He relocated Charlotte and the children to a temporary rental at Black Hawk by late Fall. The move was disastrous for Charlotte who had a recurring bout of yellow fever. She was new in the Black Hawk community and few contacts and friends while Rob was away during this illness which left her almost incapacitated with three young children under tow.

In addition, the children had been fending off bouts of whooping cough. Rob felt that his family was neglected by the Black Hawk community which precipitated some ill feelings. He immediately moved the family to the state capitol at Jackson, Mississippi.

Black Hawk, Mississippi, Sept. 23, 1848 (excerpts)

My Dear Love

My health is yet good but I have been writing all this week and getting anxious to go out again. I cannot yet tell you when I shall return to home.

I have been offered several places here at a fair price and one of them I think I shall buy for three hundred dollars. It has a double cabin, garden, kitchen smoke house and yard. The houses were built last year and are about as good as log houses generally are. The garden is good. It is just on the edge of town and about a hundred yards from the Baptist Church.

I think you will like it. I shall write a few lines to Grundy which I want you to hand to him.

I hope you are all well. My heart is with you although my body is at this place. My inward eyes behold you and I seem to hear your voice although I am so far distant from you. I shall love you I hope, as long as my heart continues to beat in this bosom and when I die I hope God will be a better friend to you than I have been.

Tell my dear children that Pa wants to come home and go down the ridge with them. He will come home someday if God will let him.

Your dear husband

R. Morris

Sharon, MS., Nov. 19, 1848 (excerpts)

My Dear Wife

I have not traveled far since I left you. This place is only a short two days ride from Black Hawk and if I could I would like to ride it tomorrow. But I must go on further and further for two months before I can see any of you again and every Sunday evening I shall feel that I am increasing my distance from my family.

I have had a slight attack of rheumatism today owing to this spell of cold weather. It is very muddy indeed, so much so that it is hard for us to get about.

We have been as successful in business thus far as we could expect and have good hopes to encourage us to go on.

Mr. Eckles, brother to Joseph and Simeon Eckles, is the teacher in charge of the Female Academy and a very agreeable man. I have made his acquaintance.

Tomorrow I leave here to go towards Jackson and you will write a letter to me at that place care of Thomas Palmer, Esq.

In the following, Morris referred to the death of Mississippi Governor Alexander McNutt, who died suddenly at the age of 46. He encouraged Charlotte to improve her penmanship and to think about a career as a teacher.

Jackson, Mississippi
Sunday, November 26, 1848 (excerpts)

My Dear Wife

I wrote to you a short letter yesterday and promised a long one today. I am sitting in Mr. Palmer's printing office which is right over the house where I board. Everybody but Wilson has gone to hear the funeral sermon of Governor McNutt. Poor man. How little he thought when we saw him at Mr. Johnson's that he was to die so soon. We must always be prepared to die for death so we will not find us disappointed as his coming.

I have continued in good health only for an occasional attack of rheumatism. Whenever I get my leg wet or cold I always suffer from that complaint but by warming it well it does not last long.

I have been thinking a good deal about your willingness to study and to spend an hour every day at it. If you are really determined to you may begin by writing. Get some paper and copy anything out of a box so as to spend one hour at it. You spell very badly and this will teach you both how to write and how to spell well.

When I come home if you have improved enough I will then lay out a course of study for you by which you could make a Teacher of yourself in three years and thus support our family comfortably in case you were left helpless.

Any woman who knows how to teach can make one hundred and fifty dollars a year and you could live well on that and educate your children.

Do think seriously about this matter. All that you need is to spend one hour practice each day. After a few weeks it will become a pleasure to you instead of trouble. May God assist you to a proper consideration by it.

I felt very thankful when I opened your letter to find that altho' the children were sick yet they were getting better and that you had not had another chill but were getting fat. You need a good deal of fat to make up your losses and I now command you to get much flesh upon your body before I return or I will scold at you.

Whenever you feel at all like a chill get some quinine and take it freely, it will stop it immediately.

I am not at all pleased at the idea of you being left alone but if you can bear it for a few weeks I will try to make the matter easier when I return. It is strange that Grundy does not write to us what he is going to do so that we may govern ourselves accordingly.

Write to me in answer to this to Gallatin and tell Mr. Guthrie to so do up to Dec. 6. Also send Mr. Watson's letters to the same point.

Give me a list of what you want in New Orleans up to $10 that is as high as I can go.

The following letters from Charlotte framed the circumstances of a miserable move to Black Hawk.

Nov. 23, 1848

I rote you a letter last week and the children was all sick but they have all got well again. I received a letter from you yesterday which was verry much pleased to see only you sayed that you would not be at home under two months that did not please me a bit. I hope that next letter I get you will say that you will be at home in two weks.

The last two days you left home was perfectly miserable but that is awaring off on me some but wont dare to suffer my self to think time much about it yet but when I think of the you will be at home I return it with great pleasure. Hop you wont come on Friday and leave on Monday. I claim four weeks the next time.

I red your letter to John last night and he lisned with a great deal of attention till I got through as he was delighted with the thoughts of his horse and wagon. He has not thought of much else since for he is all the a time a talk about it. Little sis don't talk much interest in nothing but her doll baby. She talks about par and says he will come home tomorrow. Little ally is a steping a lot and feels himself as large as anybody an hollows of often thare. Now your little ally is a sweet child but he has a reched temper.

I have my foot on the cradle a rocking him now the verry looks of his face is a pleasure to me. now about my self well I havenot had very chill since you lef here.I feels little like a chill as anything else and I don't think I will have very nother one for I haven't such ravenous apetite as I had. I took the quinine as you directed for five mornings. It used my head pretty rough ... it all most made me deranged. I could not sleep nor could nor even lie still on the bed so I set up nearly all night but it did not last long. Now I have told you all about my self that no but if you was here to night I could tell you how much I love you and I think you would believe it.

If you should go to New Orleans before you come home I want you to bring me three pounds of spun yarn and bring me a leghorn bonet and little sis a leghorn hat ... and bring me four yards of black silk and eight yards of jacknet muslin and four yards of linen

In December, Rob wrote to Charlotte that he was very upset about Charlotte and the children's welfare at Black Hawk. Rob realized the stress that he had put on Charlotte with young children as well as the sickness that has plagued the family. He discussed the move to Jackson.

Dec. 11, 1848

My Dear Charlotte

Mr. Guthrie in writing to Gillespie at this place tells a doleful account of your situation without meat without company or comfort. This is very painful to me and a great disappointment because I thought I had everything well arranged in placing you at Gillespie's house. But this has been a year of trials with you and I hope I shall live to reward you for them all ... my intention now is to take you to Jackson by stage or steamboat immediately. To board you at Mrs. Johnson's until we can get a chance to rent a small house, then to put you to housekeeping and stay at home about half the time with you. I think there will not be much difficulty in getting a house a mile or two out of town and it will not probably cost us a great deal rent. If Grundy will move down and live with us you can have company at all times.   Your husband, R. Morris

CHAPTER FIVE

A Masonic Career

In 1849, Morris continued his work selling subscriptions and traveled extensively, making another trip to the Eastern seaboard. In a letter written on August 23, 1849, he mentioned about another visit to see his brother and sister. During these years, Charlotte and the children lived in Jackson, Mississippi and Germantown, Tennessee. Another child, Robert Morris, was born on Dec. 11. 1849. Charlotte constantly worried about Morris' travels and the risk of accidents.

Steamboat travel was very popular but also very dangerous. Over 1800 people were killed from steamboat explosions during 1816-1848 in the intercontinental United States that resulted from improperly maintained and watched boilers (Hunter, 1949.) Charlotte substantiated her fear of steamboat fires in her letter written to Rob on August 2, 1849: "I haven't heard from you since you left us on the wharf and when I heard the bell ring and the boat start I felt as if it would all most kill me. I never slept one wink that night when they waked me next morning I hadn't never closed my eyes for sleep and the next night I heard that they was five boats burnt up between Memphis and Louisville and was so uneasy about it that I could not sleep nor rest in day time, but I have heard since that they was burnt at St. Louis."

Morris visited his sister and brother-in-law in Boston and did business in New York City during August 1849 where he mentioned the cholera epidemic: "The cholera is still in this city, about thirty deaths a day, but the city is so large that no body seems to miss the dead and not a word is said about the disease. People in these large towns are very cold hearted."

In 1850, the sale of subscriptions was not going as well as Morris had hoped due to a national financial crisis. This was a time in America when government was struggling with issues such as territorial expansion, sectionalism among states, and slavery. Immobilization and the lack of strong leadership from Washington created stalemates on a national consensus for most issues. Morris called that year a catastrophe in his business affairs. However, his masonic endeavors greatly advanced. He made another trip to the Eastern seaboard establishing more contacts and it was the Spring 1850 that Rob took his son, John to New York and Massachusetts to meet Uncle John and Aunt Charlotte. The following letters described their trip.

March 13, 1850 Mississippi River near Helena

Dear Wife

I write today so that I can mail this at Memphis. We are getting along finely. John say tell ma we are all well. He has made acquaintance with some little boys and girls on the boat and he plays from morning till night. Only he says his lesson once every day. He eats at the second table and eats a heap and when night comes he kneels down with Pa in our little room and prays that God will take care of us and bring us home again safe. We hope to get to New York about Saturday, March 23.

This is a small boat and has very few passengers. I am very busy writing all the time as usual. We have plenty of music on board and a monkey. Tell Sis that the monkey jumped on John and scratched his hands.

I hope that you are all in good health and that I shall see you again in six weeks. Pray for me that no harm may happen to me. Your affectionate husband

R. Morris

Louisville March 18 1850

Dear Wife

As we will get to Cincinnati tonight and I shall have no chance to write to you again before we reach New York I will write now. We are all well and John seems very happy. He has seen the high rocks and the other curiosities along the river. His last shirt is very dirty and I don't know how to get one washed for him. He lost his handkerchief yesterday and is very sorry. He wishes that you could all be here to see the beautiful Ohio River and watch the steamboats coming down and he wants Sis and Alfred to play with. I spend all my time reading and writing and I hear John's lesson every day. Yesterday he said four lessons.

You must get Mr. Houghton to punish Mary if she becomes unruly and if you cannot manage her then, send to Mr. Sloane and have her sent home.

I shall write to you again next Friday march 22 and hope to be able to say that we are all well. Farewell dear wife and forget not your husband.

John wants to put his name: John

Louisville became a steamboat center and convenient port for Morris
as he travelled up and down the Mississippi and Ohio Rivers.

Templar dress and costume items from the Rob Morris collection.
Courtesy of The Grand Chapter of Kentucky, OES.

Knight Templar Handbook composed by Rob Morris to help standardize ritual and organization. *Courtesy of The Grand Chapter of Kentucky, OES.*

Illustration from Morris's plantation novel *The Faithful Slave*.

New York March 27 1850

Dear Wife

We got here safely on the 24th. I have caught a bad cold but John is well and very happy. He has seen the ships and fountain and has been to the museum. All which was very delightful to him. On Friday the 29th we go to see Uncle John and he is quite anxious for the day to arrive. We are boarding with the kind lady who takes good care of him when I am out. She thinks John is one of the finest children in the world and wonder how we raised him so well in Mississippi. I have bought him 3 shirts and a full suit of clothes made in the New York styles and are handsome.

I shall expect to get a letter from you by tomorrow.

Kiss all our dear children and pray for us that we may be brought safely home.

Your true friend

R.Morris

John says "I shall go to ma in a few weeks."

By 1850, Morris had received degrees of the Royal Select Master, exalted to the degree of Royal Arch in Lexington, Mississippi and made Knight Templar at Jackson.

Throughout the year, Morris had made numerous contacts through his subscription business, but he had not made a lot of money. Discouraged with sales but encouraged by his relationships with masons he had met during his expansive travels, Morris was convinced that he could pursue his career as a "Teacher of Masonry" (Rule, 1922, p. 233.) He foresaw himself as a paid lecturer who would visit lodges across the United States, producing and writing Masonic journals, and unifying the masonic laws and ceremony.

During the Fall of 1850 through early summer of 1851, Morris started a series of lectures and sermons in Tennessee that solidified his position as Masonic lecturer. In November 1850 at Colliersville, Tennessee, Morris gave the first series of lectures, over a three-day period followed by a Sunday lecture before a public audience on "The Building of King Solomon's Temple." That lecture became the standard subject for hundreds of lectures to follow and as he delivered more and more lectures, he became a popular figure. He also conferred the Eastern Star degree in Colliersville and wrote to Charlotte about the enthusiastic response for the Eastern Star. He would confer the degree for her, if she so desired, when he returned home. The series of lectures from the letters to Charlotte show him at Sumerville, Middleburg, Whiteville, Purdy, Savannah, Lexington, Cotton Grove, Caledonia, Memphis, Dancyville, Covington, Brownsville, Mason Groveand Denmark, Tn. The children and Charlotte resided in Shelby County, Tennessee (Rule, 1922, p. 234.)

In the second letter from this series, Morris indicated he had priced slaves. As he traveled from north to south, economic ventures on the national scale included a deepening wedge on the use of slavery between the rising anti-slavery sentiment of the North and the South's defensiveness. Rob Morris was conflicted on the issue of slavery. As a native from Massachusetts, the institution of slavery was not a factor in his upbringing. His wife Charlotte, however, came from a slave holding family and the Morris family letters revealed that Rob promised Charlotte slaves several times to help ease the burden of housekeeping. He priced slaves in his correspondence, but he never purchased slaves. Often however, Charlotte "hired out" slaves from other owners. This was a common practice where slave owners would lease their slaves for household work, field labor, and other tasks to others. The agreement usually included that the lease provide a suit of clothes including shoes and room and board. Sometimes, slaves would be allowed to keep part of the money (Oldham County Historical Society, 1824-1864.)

Curiously, at this time, Morris wrote a short novel, *The Faithful Slave* that embellished the attributes of the slave as a faithful, dutiful, and attached member of a family. Morris began the novel with disclaimers regarding his opinion to the institution of slavery, but embellished the slave character as typified by southern romanticism, a "profound attachment, the spaniel-like devotion which so many of the Southern slaves display toward their masters' interests (p. 1)."

Later in the novel, Morris described life for a slave in the sugar plantations of Louisiana: "the term suggestive of driving labor, scanty food, restricted society, deprivation of Sabbath privileges, and early death!—that idea which to the negro brings separation from his friends, a long, hard journey under the most cruel of drivers, and a change of occupation under the severest of taskmasters (p. 1)!"

The gist of the novel followed the life of a slave girl, Loogy, who was accused of theft and accepted the accusation in order to protect her owner, Miss Caroline. As punishment, Loogy was sent to labor on a sugar plantation. Loogy almost died, but at the last moment the truth is discovered that

Miss Caroline's ruthless boyfriend was the thief and Loogy was returned to Miss Caroline to live out her life in peace.

Although Morris suggested the reader make their "own conclusions" about the institution of slavery, the moral dilemma of Loogy raises questions. The stories that depicted the enslaved through a "white" perspective became labeled as "plantation novels" and created a sympathetic audience. In retrospect and historically, plantation novels were another contribution to a growing genre of slave literature that included narratives written by former slaves such as Henry Bibb, describing the horrendous conditions of enslavement. These stories and narratives became part of the inspiration that influenced Harriet Beecher Stowe's *Uncle Tom's Cabin* of which Abraham Lincoln insisted "had really started the war (Riccards, 1997, p. 200.)"

Somerville, Feb. 28, 1851

Dear Wife

I have sent money today to Falls and Fisher at Memphis and told them to send you some sugar, coffee, apron check flour, bacon and a bedstead.

They will be sent out to Kenners Grocery and I hope you will get them next week.

My health is good. I cannot say when I shall be at home but will come as soon as I can.

I shall send some money to Falls and Fisher to pay to Francis Mendenall by the Fifteenth of March and then I will send some for you also. The best way to keep you supplied with money will be to keep it in their hands and you send our Order for as much as you need from time to time.

I will also direct all my letters to Memphis and have them left at their store so you can send there for them.

Anything in the way of Dry goods, groceries and medicines that you may want you can get by sending them an order.

I hope that you are all well. My ardent prayers are offered up day and night for your welfare and that of my dear children.

Read you bible every day and remember that there is no happiness in this world without religion.

From your faithful husband
R. Morris

Middleburg, Hardeman County, Tennessee March 4, 1851

My dear Wife

I wrote to you from Louisville Feb. 28. It is my intention now to write to you every week and I only wish I could get a letter from you so often. I priced some negro girls today, only ten years old and they asked five hundred dollars a piece. A negro woman with two little children one thousand dollars.

I hope to be able to buy you a good girl by the month of June and if I have to stay away from you until that time you must not complain. My whole wishes are to make your lot in life an easier one and to support my dear children. The way I am getting on I shall be very comfortably situated by next Christmas and then I can stay more at home. I feel very much encouraged indeed. You must pray for me and send my your good wishes night and morning.

As soon as you get this letter, sit down and write me a long letter and have it ready to send to me by the time you got my next letter. Don't let anybody see my letters nor know what I am doing or how much money I am making.

Your faithful husband
Rob Morris

Whiteville   March 20, 1852

My Dear Wife

I sent $55 last week to Falls & Fisher to pay you Ten dollars and to Frances Forty dollars and to let you have $5 worth of goods. Next week I will send you more money.

As soon as you receive this write me a letter and enclose it in the envelope I now send you.

If you have to pay a dollar to send it to Memphis or German-town be sure to send it. The easiest way to get it put into the post office will be to hand it to the stage driver as the goes by and give him 25 cts to put it in the office. I hope you will not fail to have this done so that I can get a letter form you when I get to Brownsville.

I want to know how you are getting along and all about each of the children separately.

Tell me how Wilson is and his prospects of business, also your Father's family and all the news of the neighborhood. I have not had any intelligence of your since I left you.

I feel quite bad to think it will be ten weeks before I get back. I am quite lonesome at times especially on Sunday, if I could only be at home on Sunday I would not care so much. Sometimes I distress myself by thinking that you may get sick and then what would the children do.

Then I grieve for fear the children might get sick and nobody but yourself to take care of them. Amidst all these troubles I gain great consolation by affecting upon God's goodness to us and then I push ahead as hard as I can to make money. Prospects brighten around me everyday and if I can do as well all the year as I am doing now our circumstances will be quite good.

Take good care of yourself, my love. Remember you are the only dependence at home. Better hire all your washing done than to exert yourself to as to get sick.

If you want to hire a servant at any time, do so, it will meet my consent and I will keep you in money.

I would like for John to come home every Friday evening. I don't want him to get wearied away from home. He ought to be under your eye every Saturday and Sunday. Keep the children well clothed and shod. Send for the doctor when any is sick, without delay.

You may buy John a strong hatchet when his school is out and encourage him to stay at home and take care of the children. When I send you money pay the School Bill, Kennen's bill, Davis, Bradley and three or four dollars to Francis. Don't get in debt another tie if you can help it. I am determined to go no more into debt forever.

Can't you being to teach little Charlotte her letters. I will buy her a workbox when I come home if she will know all her letters so as to say them correctly.

Buy clothing, furniture or provisions you think proper. You need a set of chairs and some ironware.

Won't you make a new resolution and read a chapter every night.Since you quit the practice your religious impressions are weakened. I hope you will begin again to do it and be sure to pray often for yourself, your husband and your children.

Pray for all the world, for we always enjoy our religion best when we feel anxious for the spirit of welfare for others.

I do most earnestly pray for you, my dear wife. We have lived long together and I have learned to think highly of your affection for me and your patient care for your children. We have met many misfortunes and mortifications and discouragements but perhaps were sent to us to try us.

Perhaps God saw that the only way to soften our hard hearts was to afflict us. Let us humble ourselves under his gracious hand and try to live so as to please him. If we do this we shall be happy no matter how much we may be afflicted.

May the Almighty keep you and guard you by day and by night. May you be preserved holy and grow in grace and in the knowledge of the Lord Jesus Christ.

May we all meet again and enjoy each others society as those can only do who love one another. May our business prosper so that we can once more settle in our own home, in our own house and not be compelled to separate so much.

And when all our labors on earth are ended may the Saviour take us in his arms and guide our souls to heaven.

Thus prays your husband

R Morris

Purday, March 26, 1851

My Dear loved Wife

I wrote to you last week at Whitesville and told you to write to me immediately to Brownsville as I shall be there in two or three weeks. I hope you have not failed to do what I requested.

My health continues good and prospects encouraging. I shall leave here tomorrow.

I am staying at Brother McKinney's a kind and good family. They have a little girl who handed me a piece of candy this morning and told me to give it to little Charlotte when I go home. I would give a pound of candy to see my little girl if only for a few minutes.

I have no news to tell you . I keep busy day and night and try to forget all troubles and cares as well as I can.

I enclose you $10 to be used in any way you think best. I will send you soe more in two weeks.

Remember me, dear wife, in prayer

Yours faithfully

R Morris

Savannah, Tennessee, March 30, 1851 (excerpt)

My Dear Charlotte

This place is on Tennessee River and steamboats pass it every day. I could get on the boat here and be with you in two days. It is quite a temptation to think of it, I do assure you. But before I get home I must make a good deal more money and if it goes hard with you when you have all the children with you, think how it must affect me, alone and unhappy, not knowing whether you are alive or well, sick or dead. It is very hard to bear you may be certain.

My health continues to be good and I am gaining flesh rapidly. I think you will find me looking much better than you have seen me for a good while.

My mare holds out very well and is also getting fat.

I quit drinking coffee about four weeks ago and think I enjoy better health. I drink water or milk, eat no meat for supper and go to bed early.

Tell John that my whiskers don't grow a bit bigger than they used to be

Comments enclosed in same letter for son John:

I suppose your school is out now and you will stay at home. You must get ma to give you some money to pay Mr. Brooks for his school bill. Schoolmasters always ought to be paid as soon as school is out. While you are home you must act pa's dear good boy and take care of the children. Keep away from the saw mill and the branch and get wood and chips for ma. Ask ma to give you some money to buy two fish lines and some hooks. When I come home we will have fine times fishing.

There is lots of Indian mounds on tops of the high hills on the bank of Tennessee River. We saw this river once when we went up the Ohio River. There is gravel here with encrimites and banded jasper and petrified wood but not one agate.

From your father, Robert Morris

Lexington, Tennessee, April 13, 1851.

My Dear and Well-beloved Wife

Again I sit down to spend a Sabbath hour in writing you a letter. It is a great pleasure to feel that although I cannot sit by your side and talk with you yet I can make my pen speak to you and in this way I can keep you informed of where I am andhow I fee. Since last Sunday I have been traveling in a very rocky, hilly country where but few people live and they mostly poor. But they are very generous, hospitable and kindhearted. They treated me so kindly that I partly promised them to come and spend a week with them next fall.

I will send you $10 next week. Pay John's school bill and all other debts that we owe in the neighborhood. Have you got time to make me two or three shirts by the first of June. I had new collars put to these three but I am afraid they will not answer until I get back. Be sure to make them large enough and put pearl buttons in the bosoms. If you cannot get time hire somebody to help you.

I shall get your letters next week at Brownsville. I am exceedingly anxious to hear from you as I have not hear a word since I left you. I suppose that Robert walks alone by this time. Don't fail to let Alfred have breeches by the time I get home. Tell little Sis to keep her hair combed and her face and hands clean. She must take good care of the baby and be Pa's good little girl.

I have been to church this morning to hear a Methodist preach a first rate sermon. It is the first Sunday that I have spent without preaching for a long time, but I shall probably be called upon to preach tonight.

I will send you some more money in two weeks. Be economical. Don't lend a cent of money to anybody nor let anybody know that you have got it. Buy everything that you need. If you have not got chairs yet you would do well to send for a set worth about $5.

And now, dear wife, accept my sincere love. My heart and affections are all your and your they shall be while life shall last.

Rob Morris

My dear John

I wanted you with me the other day when I spent a whole day in gathering flowers and shells and fossils. You never saw anything so thick as they are. Why the encrinites are so thick you could get your hat full in half an hour. And the most beautiful favosites and helixes and paludinaes. And the whole hillsides are covered with flowers of all sorts mighty pretty. There is a cave that runs under a mountain and I went into it more than a quarter of a mile deep under ground.

I promised the folks that I would come again next Fall and bring my little boy with me and we would spend a whole week there.

If you will study your book one hour every day till I get back and have the whole multiplication table perfect when I come home you shall go with me when I visit this place again. Be a good boy my dear son, and God will bless you.

I pray to god every night to take care of my dear children and make them all good. You cannot be happy unless you are good.

This is from your father.

R. Morris

Trenton, Gibson County, Tennessee, May 4, 1851

My Dear Wife

This is a wet gloomy day and I am confined to the house by the rain. I am stopping with Dr. Hess, a Cumberland minister and a worthy excellent man. He and his family have been very kind to me. Mr. Giles lives near here, the man who used to sell us bacon when we lived at Mount Sylvan. Mr. Donaldson, Elisha's father-in-law, lives about ten miles from here but I have not seen him. It is a healthy, beautiful country about here and I feel certain your would like it. The people are as different from the stingy, hardhearted folks in Mississippi as it is possible to be.

The land is good and cheap. Our denomination have a great many churches, good schools and clever folks. It is fifty miles from the Mississippi River and about one hundred and twenty from Memphis.

Last Monday was the anniversary of the death of our oldest child. I could not help thinking how afflicted we were on that occasion which is now eight years gone by. Our heavenly father has been very kind to us since that grievous day, in giving to us four in place of the one he took. May his mercy preserve them all from day to day.

This will probably be the last letter I shall write to you before I get home. I suppose you would rather see me than my letters. I am sure I would give anything I have got to spend a week or two at home for I have never been so homesick in all my life as I have during the last two months.

This is the longest absence from you that I have ever made since we were married and I find it altogether too long for my comfort.

While business is good and I am making money so fast I think it is better that we suffer some inconvenience than to be always poor and in distress. One year as the rate I am now getting on will enable us to buy a comfortable home and at least one negro woman. This will place us in a comfortable situation in life and enable us to educate our dear children and do something for the course of the Lord.

When I get home I will confer on you the Eastern Star Degrees. I have given them to more than fifty ladies since I left home and everybody is pleased with them. They are in fact very beautiful and interesting. If you want to take them you must sit down and read the 11th Chapter of Judges, the 2nd Chapter of Ruth, the 2nd Chapter of Esther, the 11th Chapter of Gospel of John and the whole of the Second Epistle of John. By reading these you will be prepared to understand the degrees.

From your husband, Rob Morris

With additional comments to John

There is a great place for fishing up here but I have not fished any but if you were with me I would go tomorrow. There is a great big lake full of fish. I killed a cottonmouth snake the other day like the one that Governor Mathews killed when we all went to get blackberries. I took a stick and tried to make him bite it but he would not bite the stick, though he opened his mouth and looked mighty mad. I don't believe a cottonmouth will bit only when he is in the water. You must find all the good places where we can dig worms to go fishing with when I come home. Get some good poles too if you know where there is any and be sure to send some money to town to buy some hooks and lines.

Be obedient to your mother and do what she tells you. Be kind and gentle with the children. Study your books every day.

From your father, Rob Morris

Dancyville, Tennessee, June 1, 1851

My very dear Charlotte

I came to Macon on the day that I left home and by night my mare got so badly foundered that she could not move till Saturday. I was afraid she would die but she is now nearly well again. I was very kindly treated at Mr. Millers but would much rather have staid at home than waited there so long. Home is a place very dear to me. I do not think that I ever enjoyed home so well in all my life as I did the last time I was with you. The happiness of that two weeks will never be erased in my memory. I feel that I am greatly indebted to you for your kindness and attention to me and for your heartfelt love which made me so happy while I was with you. God reward you, my dear wife, and may his richest blessings of peace and love be with you in the long, lonely hours of my absence. Your condition is a hard one and I truly feel sorry that it must be so. But if God shall bless us it need not always be so. The time is not far distant I hope, when we may be together in a home of our own and enjoy the society of each other more than we have done for five years. That will be a happy time for you. I know that you love to have a home of your own where you can feel settled and comfortable. I am getting very tired of moving about so much and I want to get to some place where we will not be compelled to move again.

I cannot tell exactly how long I will be away from you this trip. You may look for me only when you hear me coming. Neither can I tell you where to write me but will do so in my next letter. I have had weak eyes and sore mouth ever since I left home. Sometimes so bad that I could hardly see or eat anything. This hot weather affects me very much and am afraid it will make our children sick. If John has commenced going to school send the enclosed paper to his teacher. I expect you to do what you think proper about his boarding at your father's. Get him a slate, quill, ink and paper and slate pencils. I want him to come home every Saturday.

Kiss all the dear children for me. Tell Sis that she shall have her workbox as soon as we get our new home. Tell Alfred that I know a mighty pretty panther story that I never told him. It is about a black panther and three snakes. You must take good care of that dear little Robert for my sake. He gained by heart the last time I was at home though he did treat my coat so mean.

Good bye dear wife. God bless you. R. Morris

Comments to John (Author's comment: The Noconnah is a small river that runs from Colliersville, Tennessee to Germantown, Tennessee.)

If you go to school this summer you must learn arithmetic and learn to write. You are now getting to be a big, stout boy and it is time you learned something. I shall expect to hear that you have been a good boy and if so I will let you stay at home with me next time. We must catch all the fish in the Noconnah when I come home again and not leave a single old bullhead in it. When you are at home you must read ten verses for me every night and morning. It is mighty hot weather. Ginny got foundered the other day and like to have died. I felt mighty sorry for her. She couldn't walk a bit. She didn't eat or drink hardly anything for two days. Be a good boy.

From your father   Robert Morris

Mason Grove, Tennessee June 29, 1851

My Dear Wife

When I wrote to you last Sunday I thought I should have gone down to Belmont which is only 35 miles from you but here I am still further off and no prospect now of getting home for two months. Last Tuesday we had a great masonic celebration at Brownsville at which there was a very large company.

Today we have a splendid rain after a long dry spell. The ground had got so dry and dusty that if the rain had not come just as it did there would not have been any crops. Business is highly flattering and encouraging. I go some letters by the way of Germantown today. I hope I hear from you shortly ...

From your husband   Rob Morris

July 5, 1851

My dear husband

We are well and has bin ever since you left us and I hope that God's blessings will still remain with us. I got that letter with seven dollars in it and the one that was lost. John is still at school and learns verry fast but the teacher has not put him to riting yet. I have got him the third reader but the slate I have not yet. But I will get it as soon as I can. It is so hard for me to get any thing from Memphis.

John was at home to day and he is very well pleased with his school mates and teacher but when he has to leave us all he can't keep from criing. Sis and Pud is very lonesome when Jon leaves them for a day or two. They say they wish par would let John stay at home.

July 6, 1851

I recived to letters from you July 5th which I was glad to hear from you and you was well and your health is good. You say that you wil not be at home til September that is too long it is two long months yet let me say come home before. John was at home today and I red his letters to him and he sayed tell par that he wanted to see him and will be glad when the time comes for par to come home. Oh, I believe that your boy loves you dearly and your babes evry one. John is a good boy it is hard that they don't be with par all the time.

We are all well and I hope these blessings still remain with you. Nothin more but I remain your till death.

C. M. Morris

Denmark, Tennessee, July 6, 1851

My Dear Wife

Another Sabbath has come—how fast time flies. Last Sunday I wrote to you from Masons Grove about 20 miles from here. A sacramental meeting is going on by Old Reuben Burrow and three other preachers besides myself. My turn to preach will be tonight. Franklin Johnson is here—the man who took my place at DeSoto Academy. He has long ago quit teaching and gave to farming. He lives where John Derity did. Old Billy Gray will probably not live long. My health is good although the weather is oppressingly hot and I am confined in small, hot Lodge rooms from morning until night at lecturing.

It is just one month today since I left you but it seems very much longer. I have received one hundred and twenty dollars for my services in that time and think I shall do equally well for the next two or three months. I am more and more in favor of our moving up near Mill's Point this fall or winter. Land is cheap there now but rising fast. It is said to be healthy and is certainly a good looking country what I have seen of it. ... I don't want you to live in that out of the way place a single day longer than I can help.

They have started a Cumberland Church in Jackson since we left. Dennis is to be the pastor—he is also to preach at Sharon and Canton.

Mifflin, Tennessee, July 13, 1851 (excerpt)

My Dear Charlotte,

Having paid up nearly all my Memphis and Germantown debts

I can now begin to lay the money away in my pocket book and prepare to purchase a negro for you. I saw that you would rather I would
buy you a negro first and afterwards a home, so as I wish to please
you in this matter I have concluded to do it. ... Day after tomorrow I
go to Jackson (Tn.) still only two days ride from you but after that I
steer further North again.

Caledonia, Tennessee, July 27, 1851

My Dear Wife,

... Last night I was surprised and pleased to fall in with Mr. Ran-
dall who lived near us in our first settlement in DeSoto. He is brother in law of Washington Covington. He remembered me at once,
urged me to call and see his wife and many many kind inquiries after
you. He made a profession of religion the same day I did and has
remained a faithful Cumberland Presbyterian ever since. I think that
people are better Christians in this country than they were down in
Mississippi. They keep up meetings, sustain camp meetings and have
circuit riders and seem to love the cause of Christ greatly ...

I now send you $4.00 and shall probably send you some more
before I return home. If you do not need to use it lay it by and let
nobody know that you have it. You must pay the cost to Mr. Wilson
for his meal and for any other things that you buy. I do not like to
have you get out of money although I know you will be saving when
we get our negro girl we can then be a little more extravagant but in
the meantime every dollar counts one. Last week I got sixty dollars
in six days but this week I shall not so do well. I charge thirty dollars
for a course of lectures that takes three days and when I can make my
meetings hit so as not to lose any time it counts up very fast.

Good bye, dear partner, the Lord preserve you ...

Rob Morris

Additional comments to son John

My dear little boy

Your mother wrote to me that she had read all my letters to you
and that you wished that I could stay at home all the time. I am sure
that I wish so too. Do you remember the pieces I was writing when
I was at home the last time, called "A Month Among the Squirrels?"
Well, I sent those pieces to a newspaper in Philadelphia and the edi-

tor liked them so well he wrote to me he wants to give me $25 to let him print them in his paper. It was T. S. Arthur, the man who wrote the books that your Ma likes to read so well. I shall let him print them and send me the money, for it is a heap of money to get just for writing a few sheets of paper about squirrels.

Once there was a man took three of his children and went to a creek to catch fish. The oldest boy was most eight years old. They fished on the bank and the man only caught one fish while the boy caught two. Then they went to some big logs and the man did not catch a single fish while the little boy caught two more, so when they got home the man only had one fish and the little rascal had four. Don't you think that was might funny work?

I preached this morning standing under a tree in the woods. I have got a boil over one of my eyes that has swelled up that side of my face so I can hardly see out of it. It hurt me last night very much indeed. Study very hard dear son and be a good boy.

From your father

Robt. Morris

Nashville, Tennessee, Oct. 6, 1851

My Dear Wife

I got here yesterday. I have been very sick on the road—worse than I ever was before in all my life. By the kindness of God my life is preserved and I am getting well but I am too weak to write. You must not be alarmed about me for I am with kind friends. I left one hundred and seventy dollars for you at Falls & Fishers. Next week I will write you a long letter. My love to you and the dear children.

R. Morris

Charlotte, Tennessee, Oct. 26, 1851

Excerpt from letter written to son John

My Dear Boy John

Since I rode a great ways I was mighty sick once and didn't know that I should ever see my dear children any more. And as I lay in my bed with the hot fever on me and thought how sorry you would all be to hear that I was dead, the tears rolled out of my eyes. ... Nashville is a big place. The governor lives here—I saw him one day. He has got a fat, red face. When I was there Ginny (the horse) ran away, went clear out of town about six miles and was gone two days before they caught her. She was hungry enough when she got back because she had not had anything to eat in all that time.She is the greatest horse to eat that I ever saw ...

Camden, Tennessee, Nov. 2, 1851

My Dear Wife

... It seems as if I cannot get my health again for last night I had a fever and today am taking quinine to try to stop it. Tomorrow I shall commence on a regular course of strong medicines such as Blue mass for my liver is in a bad state and I cannot cure myself until I get that right. The foot has got sound and well.

At the end of 1851 the stage was set for Rob Morris to be a force in freemasonry. By visiting small Masonic lodges and churches and travelling extensively to the Northeast, Morris had generated a network of influential leaders that included judges, governors, attorney generals, senators, businessmen and even Presidents of the United States. Morris was likeable; he was a devout Christian and a prolific writer who generated poems that could document Masonic events. Morris gained the respect of fellow masons by producing poetry for cornerstone dedications, funerals, grand lodge meetings and other celebrations of sorts. He was enthusiastic for the establishment of more Masonic colleges and institutions. Morris was ready and eager to contribute to the Masonic order.

Morris developed the degrees that would become the basis for the Order of the Eastern Star. At the same time he established a Conservator Movement for Freemasonry. Freemasonry's reputation had been damaged from most vicious attack that began with an incident in 1826. William Morgan in Batavia, New York, teamed up with a printer named David Cade Miller, and two other men, John Davids and Russell Dyer, to publish the book that would reveal the "secrets of masons" (Morris, 1883.)

The attack had reverberations throughout the world of freemasonry and Morris was determined to set the organization back on the right track. The Order of the Eastern Star and the desire to standardize Masonic rituals with the Conservator Movement provided a cohesive framework that would allow freemasonry to survive and flourish into the 20th Century.

Example of a lecture program that featured Rob Morris as guest speaker. *Courtesy of The Grand Chapter of Kentucky, OES.*

CHAPTER SIX

The Conservator Period

In 1826, William Morgan viciously attacked freemasonry and threatened to publish a book to debunk the secrets of the order. The motivation for the book supposedly occurred when he was rejected as a member for a new Masonic lodge proposed in Batavia, NY. The print shop for the new book was "mysteriously" burned down and a series of events followed that jeopardized Morgan. On September 11, 1826, William Morgan was arrested for stealing a shirt and tie and taken to a jail in Canandaigua, NY. He was soon released for lack of evidence, but immediately re-arrested for failure to pay a $2.69 debt to an innkeeper. On September 12, a group of men came and paid Morgan's fine. As they took him away, Morgan was heard hollering "Murder" (Morris, 1883.)

A body was recovered from Lake Ontario presumably that of Morgan. Several inquests were made concerning the body that washed upon the shore of Lake Ontario. In one inquest, Morgan's wife positively identified the body of that being her husband. In another inquest, the body was identified as another man. Fifty-four masons were indicted for Morgan's kidnapping and of those ten masons, including the Niagara County Sheriff, Eli Bruce, were given sentences ranging from 30 days to 28 months (Ibid.)

Because Morgan's death was never confirmed, murder charges were never brought. That is one side of the Morgan story. What followed the disappearance of William Morgan was an incredible journey of tales and stories that resulted in a wave of popularity across the United States. William Morgan became a character similar to our modern day Kilroy or Waldo. He was everywhere and nowhere; was he dead or was he alive? He would appear as a sea captain in Smyrna selling fruit or was he the celebrated Indian chief, San Procope of a native American tribe who confessed on his death bed that he was William Morgan. Or, was he that man in Russellville, Kentucky who died in 1840, confessing he was the notorious Morgan. A mariner swore that he saw William Morgan as a passenger that sailed to Holland in a respectable mercantile selling gin.

Some said that a group of freemason's murdered Morgan, others said it was a rue by anti-masons to fuel support for a new political third party. Nevertheless, the event around William Morgan activities raised a notion of "skepticism" and support for those who were critics of freemasonry. It resulted in the anti-Masonic political party that created a third-party candidate for President of the United States, William Wirt. Wirt ran against Andrew Jackson (a mason) in 1832. Jackson, running for the second term in office had 219 electoral votes, popular vote of 701,780, Henry Clay who represented the Republican Party, had 49 electoral votes, 401,285 popular votes and Wirt received 7 electoral votes, 101, 715 votes (Peters, 2014.)

As the tale of William Morgan weaved itself through the next few decades jeopardizing freemasonry's organization, Rob Morris began a movement, The Conservator Movement, to standardize Masonic practices across the United States. Morris thought that standardizing masonic practices would minimize scandals like the William Morgan incident. Morris felt that the individual grand lodges of every state had compromised standard rituals. These rituals had been set into place by the original system of masonry established by William Preston in the lodges of Great Britain, Scotland, and Ireland. Thomas Smith Webb had published the first *Monitor* in the United States in 1795 to correspond with the Prestonian system and it was known as "The Webb Work." Unfortunately, Webb died in 1819 and the scandalous activities that occurred during the 1820s resulted in the decay of these standard practices. The Conservator Movement would help to re-establish the work of Thomas Smith Webb. Morris adhered fervently to the Webb work and pursued the opportunity to incorporate the Webb work on several levels, through lectures, publications, and establishment of Masonic schools.

The first well-known and most popular book on this subject was *The Lights and Shadows of Free Masonry consisting of Masonic Tales, Songs and Sketches* in 1852. (See Appendix A) The book was written in a light-hearted narrative style that Morris generated "from a large collection of facts, gathered in my travels through almost every section of the United States." Each chapter of the book dealt with a particular story that underscored the relevance of freemasonry and its importance for day-to-day living. The first chapter, "Death on the Sierra Nevada", focused on the life of Laban Tolliver, a Mason who under unfortunate circumstances lost his investments that supported his family. Tolliver set out to find gold in California. He died on his journey but was not alone because he traveled with masonic brethren who saw that he was buried with Masonic honor.

Another story related how a mason, captured by Indians, was spared death at a burning stake when rescued by the Indian chief. The chief had received Masonic instruction in the past and recognized a Masonic breastpin, worn by the prisoner. Other chapters included tributes to Eastern Star degrees,

THE

LIGHTS AND SHADOWS

OF

FREEMASONRY.

CONSISTING OF

MASONIC TALES, SONGS, AND SKETCHES,

NEVER BEFORE PUBLISHED.

BY ROB. MORRIS, K.T.,
LECTURER ON THE LANDMARKS AND WORK OF FREEMASONRY.

LOUISVILLE, KY.,
PUBLISHED BY J. F. BRENNAN, FOR THE AUTHOR.
1852.

Inside cover of *Lights and Shadows of Freemasonry* by Morris, in humorist genre, which typified a rise of the new authors defining American literature.

J. F. Brennan, whose printing house was located on First and Market Street in Louisville, was a good friend and publisher of Rob Morris.

Morris published his Almanac to give Masons day to day
guidance on Masonic rituals and organizations.

The advertisement shows the various publications available from Morris &
Monsarrat, "Publishers of Masonic Intelligence" on 472 Main Street in Louisville.

adulations of exemplary masons and lodges, and a question and answer chapter on "Catechism of Masonry." The catechism chapter included questions such as "What is Masonry", "What was the origin of speculative Masonry among men?", "What is Operative Masonry?" and so on.

The "catechisms" of masonry from this work are expanded, repeated, and organized into various publications that Morris produced in Masonic newspapers and journals. He gave suggestions on how to run a local lodge and conduct proper order, often explaining the historic traditions that gave meaning to ritual. Readers were encouraged to write to Morris on questions of freemasonry order and etiquette such as how to get rid of a lodge member or proper dress and presentation for specific events. Morris established a friendship with J. F. Brennan who operated a Masonic printing press in Louisville. With Brennan's help, they began a semi-monthly magazine *The Kentucky Freemason* that later morphed into *The American Freemason*.

Morris produced detailed lists of the established lodges in the United States with their locations and membership in his book *Prudence of Freemasonry for 1859*. The intention was to make these lists updated and annual, but the process was not quite tangible enough to make it a successful endeavor. As Morris described the purpose of the book and explained its title: "You are cautiously to examine a strange brother in such a manner as PRUDENCE shall direct you, that you may not be imposed upon by an ignorant, false pretender, whom you are to reject with contempt and derision, and beware of giving him any hints of knowledge."

The sheer volume of work that Morris produced during this period is difficult to assess. Publications included *Masonic Book of the Americas* that focused on Eastern Star degrees, The *History of Kentucky Masonry*, The *Freemason's Almanacs*, and *Odes for Masonic Occasions*, a series of poems that were later expanded into several books, and numerous articles submitted to various print sources.

During the early 1850s, Morris established an office at 472 Main Street in Louisville with D. T. Monsarrat where he sold Masonic Publications such as *Sherer's Masonic Degree Book*, The *Gems of Masonry*, *The Freemason's Monitor* by Thomas Webb Smith, *The Voice of Masonry* and *Tidings from the Craft*, a newspaper edited and published by Morris and *The Universal Masonic Library*. Lithographs, such as "View of Jerusalem as Besieged by Titus" and "View of Solomon's Temple" were sold along with items such as Sherer's "Masonic carpets" which could be used in lodges as part of décor and ritual.

Louisville proved to be a great location for Morris as a central stop from his frequent travels between north and south. With the opening of the first canal in the United States in 1832, the Portland Canal, steamboats were able to effectively traverse the distance between Pittsburgh to New Orleans. Louisville gained prominence as a popular shipping port that also included one of the largest ports for steamboat manufacturers, the Howard Steamboat Company.

A dark period during the 1850s for Morris was his association with Jonathon Leonard, a publisher in New York who partnered with Morris to raise funds for the publication of *The Universal Masonic Library*. Morris felt that *The Universal Masonic Library,* would be the coup d' gras for a universal standard of Masonic ritual. The library would consist of 53 standard works published in 30 volumes, each handsomely bound in leather at the price of $50. Each lodge would purchase the library and the work could be the reference standard as lodges conducted their business. The volumes proposed were impressive and in order to publish the works, Morris partnered with Jonathon Leonard to collect subscriptions from lodges across the United States which resulted in over $125,000 of pledges.

Unfortunately, there was a national financial crisis in 1857 that resulted in a default of credits and loans. Leonard had mismanaged funds and Morris was left in tremendous debt. A friend of Morris, William M. Ellison in Hickman, Kentucky, took over the property, copyrights, stock of books, and became agent for the creditors of Morris. Morris lost thousands of dollars in personal liabilities. Thousands of others faced financial ruin during this crisis; fortunately. Morris' contacts and reputation allowed him to continue his career.

On a personal level, Charlotte and Rob had moved their family in 1852 in a new cabin, in far western Kentucky, built by Charlotte's brother, Francis Mendenhall. The cabin was located in a rural area between Fulton, Kentucky (a railroad town) and Hickman, Kentucky (a river port on the Mississippi).

The home was close to the Union Church as well as a grist mill and was called Lodgeton. Morris moved his Masonic membership to Hickman, Mills Point Lodge, No. 120 where he remained as member for seven years. He commented, " he never saw Brotherly Love, Relief and Truth more truly displayed in the lives of the membership and community." (p. 236, Rule) There was a brief period where the family moved to Louisville on 17th and Chestnut during 1853, but they only stayed a few months and then returned to their cabin at Lodgeton.

Louisville became a popular steamboat port and a convenient stop for Morris as he travelled up and down the Mississippi and Ohio Rivers.

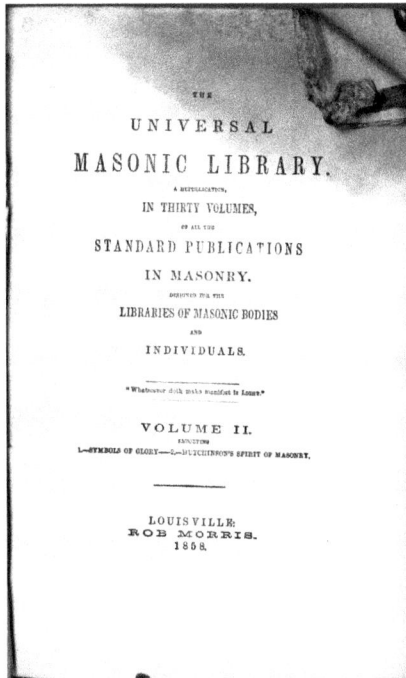

Volume 11, *Symbols of Glory and Hutchinson's Spirit of Masonry*, is an example of the 30 books that comprised The Universal Masonic Library edited by Morris.

THE UNIVERSAL MASONIC LIBRARY.

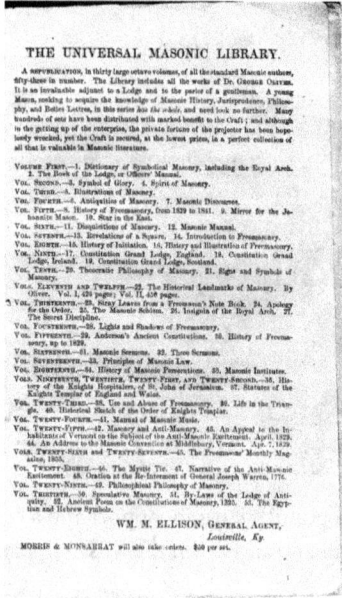

The Universal Masonic Library was Morris's attempt to provide a complete literary composition of Masonic history, jurisprudence, philosophy and "Belle" letters to educate Masons about "their" craft.

On this letterhead, Morris writes "American Freemason Editorial Office, Lodge, P.O., Fulton, Ky 1855. A post office stop was established at his home because of the volume of letters received.

The Morris added new members to their family, Robert Morris (b. Dec. 11, 1849), Sarah Mendenhall Morris (b. Jan. 28, 1852), and Ruth Electa Morris (b. July 26, 1855). John, Charlotte, and Alfred were now old enough to help with household duties when their father traveled. John frequented the local grist mill, sometimes earning extra money there, catching up on news and activities in the community. Life for Charlotte had eased up and even though she still faced the difficulties of managing a household (disease, physical work of housework, and providing family meals each day) life was better in their new home. Morris' reputation had added to the family's notoriety, and his activities generated a lot of visits from guests all over the United States. Large-scale state and national Masonic events were held in their new community in the latter part of the decade.

The Grand Lodge of Kentucky embraced Morris and Morris was quickly elected the Junior Grand Warden of Kentucky in 1855 and achieved the title of Grand Master of the Bluegrass State in 1858. He had earned these titles from the Grand Lodge with his work in 1854 on a system of "Model By-Laws" for Kentucky that he hoped would serve as a national standard (Rule, 1922.)

In 1859, the Morris family made a final move from Lodgeton to a rental house in Louisville. Morris was a well-known figure as a Masonic lecturer, writer, publisher, and poet.

The Order of the Eastern Star was growing and had seemed to overcome initial criticism regarding its place as a Masonic organization. The following are selected letters from 1852 through 1859.

Henry County, Tennessee, Feb. 15, 1852

Dear Wife

I send you $44 which you are to use in this way, keep as much of it for yourself as you need and pay the rest over to Mr. Duffey. I shall have some more in a few days.

My health continues good. I hope to find all of my dear family well when I return and the little Sarah getting large enough for me to see her.

You must not let the children go with wet feet in this weather. Let them keep their shoes and stockings dry or if they get wet they should go immediately to the fire and dry them. There is great danger in wet feet.

John must not leave his studies until noon. Git Francis to help him along and look over his studies yourself so as to encourage his mind.I think that he will make a good scholar. Tell him that as soon as Sis learns her letters he shall have his knife.

Your affectionate husband Rob Morris

April the 24th, Satterday night

My Dear Husband

We are all in tolerable health but the Baby it is sick and I don't know what can be the matter of it. It appears to have a bad cold but I do not think that is all that ales it poor little thing. I don't think it is not long for this world. I love it and I am sitting over it to night with a heavy heart. Any thing is as still as death in the room. No one nows my feelings but me and God alone what a trial it is to have a sick child and no kind of friend near. I feel to night if you was with me all would be well.

Mr. Gilbert is with us to night and I learned from him that you was well and is good spirits. I am glad to hear that you are doing so well. He told me you had some notion of going up the river and you might come by home if you can I would be glad. It is near mid night and I am still holding my sick baby.

Nothing more but think of yours Charlotte Morris

On Steamboat Columbian, June 20, 1852

My dear wife

I commence to write you a letter every Sunday. My health is good. I expected to get to Louisville last night but there was too much fog and now the whole Sunday will be spent on the boat for we will not get there before night.

There is not much cholera on this river and none on this boat. I got a subscriber for my new book from the clerk of this boat who is a Mason, and he paid me a dollar without ever seeing the book merely by my description of it. He thinks every mason will take it and as he has extensive acquaintances he will help me a good deal at various places. Now this encourages my mind a great deal I got a letter from Robinson the other day. He will pay the balance he owes me in a few days. He is going to Ohio this summer. He says every body want my book soon as it come out.

The state historical marker on Hwy. 94 between Fulton and
Hickman Kentucky identifies the Morris family log home site.

The crossing on the Mississippi River at Hickman, Kentucky where Rob
Morris often caught steamboats while the family lived at Lodgeton.

I wish Francis to go to Mills Point every Saturday evening. Let him take out my letters and open them in Mitchells store. If there is money in one (as there shall be from Robinson) he may hand that money to Mitchell the whole of it. I don't wish any one to read the letters. Let him seal them all up again and put them back in the post office. After the one comes form Robinson he had not take out any more letters for me. If any letters come to me from Hunt or Felix or any of your folks keep them. Good bye my loving wife. May heaven keep you and may we meet again in due time. Rob

Louisville, July 4, 1852 (excerpt)

My Dear Wife

I have just got through dinner and sit down to my Sunday letter. It is the next best thing to being at home this writing to dear friends at home.

It is almost like taking your hand and kissing your cheek and sitting by your side—it is almost like taking little baby on one arm and big baby on the other and playing roundings with them while the other three pull my legs and run about and holler like monkeys. But it is not quit the thing itself and so I wish I was at home today making up a part of your flock.

I have spent a laborious week and have done well. My book has been done for three days, that is one number of it – there will be four numbers. The other three will be finished before Christmas. I will send you a copy tomorrow.

The merchants here gave me a great many advertisements to put in my circular and I have made in that way, in two weeks, two hundred and forty dollars for things that will not cost me thirty. This is even better than I expected and if I do as well the next two weeks it will be making five hundred dollars in one month.

These advertisements are to be paid for in the fall and in various kinds of goods such as dry goods, a cooking stove, jewelry, clothing, carpets, medicines, a large map, silk, pictures and picture frames, farming tools, music, saddler and a great many other things. But you can see by traveling the advertisements on the cover and in the back of the book that I will send you.

My health is excellent. I get breakfast at 7 o'clock, run around until eleven, then get some coffee and bread and butter then run till half past one which is dinnertime. Supper is half past seven and to bed at eleven. I board at the Commercial Hotel at one dollar a day. I have a room to myself. I have lectured here only one night yet. Write to me again when you receive this for I shall be here some time. Yours affectionately. Rob Morris

Newcastle, Kentucky, July 25, 1852 (excerpt of letter)

My Dear Wife

It was on Wednesday on July 21 that I came out here some twenty five miles. When I shall leave or which way I shall go next is not yet decided but my next Sunday's letter will inform you. In the meantime I hope to recover my health again, for which I am taking quinine and rhubarb and have been lying still doing nothing for three days. I ought not to travel in this hot weather. Another summer I hope to stay at home, for it is very injurious to my health.

The following was written to one of Rob's publishers in Louisville, Mr. Brennan.

Hickman, Ky August 11, 1852

Dear Brother Brennan

You will pity me when I tell you I was twelve days and nights coming here, add to that three different boats.

I feel vexed and grieved at your misfortune about the mishap. I never want money so much as when a little of it would be so useful to a friend. But that I know your indefatigable character and feel confident you have worked through this difficulty somehow I should despair.

My Agents are working as good speed here as expected. Seven masonic magazines have arrived all of them praising the Lights and Shadows, some of them almost extravagantly.

I shall be back by the Grand Lodge meeting. Have no fears but what I can meet Morgan's book and hope to be able to return a part of the favor for which I am indebted to you, besides. I expect to make up the amount for Morton and Griswold the first of next week. Will write you again. The family is fine health.

Rob Morris.

January 30th, 1853

My Dear Husband

We are all well but the health of the neighborhood is bad. Mr. Calvert's black girl is dead and mr. Milburn is not expected to live and I could name a dozen more. I don't know how soon our time will come. Old Bill got away from John last night and I don't know whare he has gone to and I don't know what to do about it.

This is Sunday and a lonesome it is to. The children is all a lying on the carpet enjoying them selvs how light harted a child is ,nothin trobels them.

Mr. Merrywether told you that he and mr. Calvert had taken possession of me and the children. I don't what made him say so for I have not seen him but once since you left home.

You sayed that I mast tell you whether I needed groceries or not. I don't need any thing of the sort and money I can do with out but if you can you may send a dollar or two but I had rather you would come and bring it yourself. You stil say that you will be at home until the first of March. I can't wait that long. I don't think that will be treating me very kind when you left home I did not expect you be gone more than five or more Sundays. I was never so much this disappointed in my life but come home and I will forget, all that I want to see you soon now than ever in my life.

Your wife Charlotte Morris.

Westpoint, Kentucky, November 20, 1853 (excerpt of letter)

My Dear Wife

... I called at our house in Chestnut Street and found everything in good order. I did not have time to pack up our things and as I do not know when I shall go back to Louisville it may be next Spring before I can get them home. There has been a protracted meeting going on all this week at our church. The audiences are large and attentive and I hope much good will be done. Brother Bird has been very sick with the jaundice. His daughter Anna has gone to Macon to school to Mrs. Miller. Our business at Louisville is going on well. We got more than two hundred subscribers last week by mail. I have commenced my lecturing at this place and think I shall make a great deal of money. I bought a horse and buggy so when I get home you and the children can all take a ride. If you see Brother Merriwether soon tell him that I will send him some money next week. I shall pay him up as fast as I can ...

Lodgeton December 9nth 1853

My Dear Husband

We are all well but the baby her face and neck is broke out until it is right raw all over. Ther is no use to right about only mr. Bushart is moved and Mr. Hill has rented the place to some one else and he is not a going to tend your ground and the sistern is not begun yet. The chimney is done. Mr. Beard begins to feel mity anxious about that little note of yours. He has bin here several times already to no if you said anything about it. Bushart has not cut any wood yet nar any body ever went to mill yet. The corn is held.

The old cow has gone back to meed creek the yearlings is doing well. We are doing tolerably well. John has not got any letter ready for you yet him and Alfred is all the time in the woods. They go to Sunday school. Robert still talks about his ten sents yet.

Brother Merrywether has not sold out yet an didn't hear any talk over himself and family are well. Brother Calvert and family are well . I got the box that you sent. All was right, nothing was broke but three plates. The children all say to tell pa they want to see him but rob he say he wants pa to come home. Write to us when you will be at home for that is a time anxiously look for with us all. I have not-got but one letter from you yet and that was written on the 24th. The health of the neighborhood is good my prayers for you. Charlotte Morris

Keysburg, Kentucky, May 14, 1854 (excerpt)

My Dear Charlotte

After two weeks of suffering I find myself this morning well and free from pain. The swelling in my face which I was afraid would burst outside and make an ugly scar broke inside of my mouth and is now well. I still have some rheumatism in my right hand but not much and feel in better spirits ... Mr. Brennan has offered me three thousand dollars for my share in the Freemason next year and I want to stay at home to edit it ... from your affectionate husband

Louisville, Kentucky Sept. 5, 1858 (excerpt)

My Dear Old Wife

  I hope this finds you in good health surrounded by the dear company whom Pa so fondly loves. I cannot come home yet for I am not ready but oh how I should like to see and embrace you one by one. With Ella and Ruth upon my knee with Rob and Alf on each side, with Sarah sitting by, with Charlotte and John to close the circle and with their dear mother in the low chair before me how happy I could be this hour. Well, well, a few weeks more and I never intend to be separated from you any more ... I have walked today down to corner of Chestnut and 17th St. looking at a large and fine house, the only objection to which is the distance. It would wait till you get here before renting a house at all. I wish you were here now and the labor over ... Get all your affairs ready so that we can pack up without delay. Mr. Cook is here and will probably stay here with me. Farewell loving wife and children.

  May God keep and bless you all. R.M.

CHAPTER SEVEN

The Order of the Eastern Star

On July 19 and 20, 1848, the First Women's Rights Convention was held at the Wesleyan Chapel in Seneca Falls, New York. Up until this time, the women's movement was on a parallel course with abolitionists against slavery. Although these two movements had similar issues, their separation was important for clarity and advancement in both regards. The Declaration of Sentiments issued at the Convention declared that even though the Constitution of the United Stated declared that all are equal, there was a "long train of abuses and usurpations" of "patient sufferance's of the women under this government." Included in this Declaration were facts or complaints such as inability to vote, lack of access to fair wages, employment and educational opportunities, and inequality in laws of marriage with deeds, titles, possessions including children's guardianship to be in favor of the husband. "In view of the unjust laws" as stated in this Declaration, women "feel themselves aggrieved, oppressed, and fraudulently deprived of their most sacred rights" and insist "they have immediate admission to all the rights and privileges which belong to them". The Declaration was signed by both men and women including Abolitionist Frederic Douglas (Declaration of Sentiments, July 20, 1848.)

As the Declaration of Sentiments was being developed, Rob Morris penned the details of the initiatory degrees for the Order of the Eastern Star. Historically known as the First Era of the Order of the Eastern Star under Morris' creation, his vision for this organization could not have come at a more important time in history for the women's movement in the United States. It provided an opportunity for women to gather within the realm of an established men's fraternity across America, allowing them instant access to an established place, the Masonic lodges, and gave them a voice that connected them to a national framework of organization that was well established within local communities.

Morris saw the introduction of women into Masonic organizations as a way to improve Masonry. Freemasons "inspire philanthropy" and Morris felt women were more empathetic to the causes of widows and destitute children. "If committees of charitable women, female members of the families of Freemasons, would but undertake our charitable disbursements, the widow, the orphan and the destitute need no longer suffer neglect upon the plea that 'such oversight is not the proper work of men'"(Kenaston,

1917, p. 19.) Women would also help "keep the Lodge rooms in better condition" according to Morris (Ibid.) Perhaps the most important part of Morris' vision for the Eastern Star was to broaden the opportunities for women in the workforce as he stated:

> And there is another practical result of the Eastern Star movement, the credit of which I am in no wise inclined to give to others; this is the broader opening that is offered to females for self-support. The deadly needle, the unwomanly washtub, the unwholesome country school, the sinew-wearying kitchen, are not now the only fields on which women, old and young, who are wrestling with the perplexities of human life, can win bread. Thousands and tens of thousands of places, cleanly, womanly, easy, and fairly profitable, have been opened to them since the story of the "Five Heroines of the Eastern Star" was first disseminated in 1850. In almost every post office and courthouse throughout the lands-in a great number of banks and libraries- at the desk of cashiers of mercantile houses-behind counters-but the catalogue need not be extended. Long as it is, it is daily lengthening, and every year the salaries of women are brought more nearly to those of men, as it is found they are equally accurate and expert in business, and that the defalcations, forgeries, and general rascalities with which our morning papers are defiled are commonly the work of men, rarely of women (Kenaston, 1917, p. 24.)

Morris was intuitive for the times and his efforts reflected the major initiatives of the objectives in the 1848 Declaration of Sentiments. The Eastern Star offered a network for women whereby "many methods would be opened to women for self-support that are now sealed up. Many a clerkship, many a copyist's desk, many a situation in a post office, library, public bureau, etc. now filled by men alone, would be equally available to women" (op. cit., p. 19.)

Rob Morris was by no means the first to introduce adoptive masonry for women. According to Morris' biographer Dr. Thomas R. Austin in a *Well Spent Life* (1876): "One thing is known to all readers of Masonic literature in America: that numerous degrees in which both sexes are admitted were in use among us long before Dr. Morris' day. The *Heroine of Jericho, The Se-*

cret Monitor, *The Masons Daughter, The Good Samaritan, The Ark and Dove,* and others. Dr. Morris merely used his privilege as a Masonic teacher to invent and put into use other degrees of the same class but far superior in merit" (p. 17.)

This is a copy of a signet designed by daughter Charlotte Fales Morris of the Order of the Eastern Star. *Courtesy of The Grand Chapter of Kentucky, OES.*

Annie Pond, Grand Secretary of the Order of the Eastern Star in New York, collected rare books on adoptive masonry. She summarized her findings from these collections *Interesting Historical Data.* The earliest collection was *The Thesauros of the Ancient and honorable order of the Eastern Star as Collected and Arranged by the Committee, and Adopted by the Supreme Council in convocation Assembled May 1793.* This particular copy, which is the only one known, to date, came from Rob Morris' library. Morris gave the copy to his friend Robert Macoy, who was Morris' predecessor for continuing and expanding the Order of the Eastern Star in the 1860s. In the preface to the Third Edition of the Thesauros (1819) it stated "During the Revolutionary War and the last war with England it tended greatly to soften barbarous strife, by bringing to the aid of the wounded, the gentle charity of enlightened sisterhood."

In the preface to the Fifth Edition (1847) of the Thesauros, there are hints of connections to France from George Washington's friend the Marquis de LaFayette: "The testimony of our faithful friend and Brother Protector, Gen. Lafayette, concerning its influence during the long continental wars of Napoleon and the evidences preserved by our remaining revolutionary patriots, are too precious to be cast away in the strife which our enemies would raise. The light is again kindled, and should be sustained by every lover of good order" (Pond, 1950, p. 11.) The secret work and cabalistic acronym "F.A.T.A.L." given in the Thesauros, became the motto for the Order of the Eastern Star.

Morris in several publications acknowledges the Thesauros as well as the fact that the Degrees for the Order of the Eastern Star had historic precedence: "This degree is of French extraction, and has all the embellishments of that fanciful race. It is properly conferred in a regular organization styled a Constellation which in its American form will be shortly placed before the public" (op. cit., p. 19.)

Morris also acknowledged his awareness of ladies masonry and was conferred, along with his wife, Charlotte the Degree of Heroine of Jericho: "When I was initiated in Masonry I received my Third Degree from Brother William H. Stevens afterwards Grand Master of Mississippi. He was a Mason of considerable ability, burning zeal, and a warm advocate of Ladies Masonry. In 1847 he conferred upon Mrs. Morris and myself, the Degree of Heroine of Jericho and from him I acquired my first appetite for this whole system of Adoptive Masonry"(op. cit., p. 14.)

In later years, Morris wrote his recollections about how he came across the idea for the Order of the Eastern Star and gave a history and credit for some of the basic tenets he used as follows:

> In the winter of 1850 I was a resident of Jackson, Missis-
> sippi. For some time previous I had contemplated, as hint-
> ed above, the preparation of a Ritual of Adoptive Mason-
> ry, the Degrees then in vogue appearing to me poorly con-
> ceived, weakly wrought out, unimpressive and particular-

ly defective in point of motive. I allude especially to those Degrees styled the Mason's Daughter, and the Heroines of Jericho. But I do expressly except from this criticism, the Good Samaritan, which in my judgment possesses dramatic elements and machinery equal to those that are in the Templar's Orders, the High Priesthood, the Cryptic Rite, and other organizations of Thomas Smith Webb. I have always recommended the Good Samaritan, and a thousand times conferred it in various parts of the world.

About the first of February, 1850, I was laid up for two weeks with a sharp attack of rheumatism, and it was this period which I gave to the work in hand. By the aid of my papers and the memory of Mrs. Morris, I recall even the trivial occurrences connected with the work, how I hesitated for a theme, how I dallied over a name, how I wrought face to face with the clock that I might keep my drama within due limits of time, etc.

The name was first settled upon The Eastern Star.

Next the number of points, five, to correspond with the emblem on the Master's carpet. This is the pentagon, "The signet of King Solomon," and eminently proper to Adoptive Masonry. From the Holy Writings I culled four biographical sketches to correspond with my first four points, namely, Jephthah's Daughter (named Adah for want of a better) Ruth, Esther, and Martha. These were illustrations of four great congeries of womanly virtues, and their selection has proved highly popular. The fifth point introduced me to the early history of the Christian Church, where, amidst a noble army of martyrs, I found many whose lives and death overflowed the cup of martyrdom with a glory not surpassed by any of those named in Holy Writ. This gave me Electa, the "Elect Lady, " friend of St. John, the Christian woman whose venerable years were crowned with the utmost splendor of the crucifixion.

The colors, the emblems, the floral wreaths, the esotery proper to these five heroines, were easy of invention. They seemed to fall ready made into my hands. The only piece of mechanism difficult to fit into the construction was the cabalistic motto, but this occurred to me in ample time for use (Kenaston, 1917, p. 20.)

There is discretion in Morris' recollection about conferring the degrees to his neighbors and wife. In *Voice of Masonry* (May 1862) Morris states: "My first regular course of lectures was given in November 1850 at Colliersville, Tennessee. At Colliersville likewise I conferred the degrees of the Eastern Star and Good Samaritan. Both of these I had received some years before. The restrictions under which the Eastern Star was communicated to me were that it should only be given to Master masons, their wives, widows, sisters and daughters, and only when five or more ladies of the classes named were present; these rules I have always adhered to" (Pond, 1950, p. 19.)

On May 4, 1851, Rob wrote to Charlotte from Trenton, Tennessee in Gibson County. In this letter, he mentioned that he conferred the degrees on more than fifty ladies which substantiated his statement from the *Voice of Masonry*:

Trenton, Gibson County, Tennessee, May 4, 1851

My Dear Wife

This is a wet gloomy day and I am confined to the house by the rain. I am stopping with Dr. Hess, a Cumberland minister and a worthy excellent man. He and his family have been very kind to me. Mr. Giles lives near here, the man who used to sell us bacon when we lived at Mt. Sylvan. Mr. Donaldson, Elisha's father-in-law, lives about ten miles from here but I have not seen him. It is a healthy, beautiful county about here and I feel certain you would like it. The people are different from the hard hearted, stingy people in Mississippi as it is possible for people to be. The land is good and cheap. Our denomination have a great many churches, good schools and clever folks. It is fifty miles from the Mississippi River and about one hundred and twenty from Memphis.

Last Monday was the anniversary day of the death of our oldest child. I could not help thinking how afflicted we were on that occasion which is now eight years gone by. Our heavenly father has been very kind to us since that grievous day, in giving to us four in place of the one he took. May his mercy preserve them all from day to day.

This will probably be the last letter I shall write to you before I get home. I suppose you would rather see me than my letters. I am sure I would give anything I have got to spend a week or so at home for I have never been so homesick in all my life as I have during the last two months.

This is the longest absence from you that I have ever made since we were married and I find it altogether too long for my comfort. While business is good and I am making money so fast I think it is better that we suffer some inconveniences than to be always poor and in distress. One year at the rate I am now getting on will enable us to buy a comfortable home and at least one negro woman. This will place us in a comfortable situation in life and enable us to educate our dear children and do something for the cause of the Lord.

When I get home I will confer on you the Eastern Star Degrees. I have given them to more than fifty ladies since I left home and everybody is pleased with them. They are in fact very beautiful and interesting. If you want to take them you must sit down and read the 11th Chapter of Judges, the 2nd Chapter of Ruth, the 5th Chapter of Esther and the 11th Chapter of the Gospel of John and the whole of the Second Epistle of John. By reading these you will be prepared to understand the degrees.

From your husband
Rob Morris

The recollections of Morris wherein one instance he stated, "the degrees were conferred first with his wife and neighbors", and then in the letter stated that he "gave them to fifty ladies in his visit to Tennessee before conferring them to his wife" are conflicted. At Smith Park in Jackson, Mississippi, a monument declared the degrees first given at that particular site. But, the authentic letter written by Morris from Trenton, Tennessee to Charlotte, clarified that moment. The recollections of conferring the degrees to his wife and neighbor were written some thirty years later by Morris and can be justified as what they were "recollections." The monument at Smith Park does mark the proximity of the Morris' household when they lived in Jackson.

The influence of female masonry and various degrees that had been established before Morris' development of the Eastern Star Degrees certainly influenced Morris, but the manner and style is "distinctly original" and from Morris' hand. The time at which Morris created the Eastern Star Degrees was ripe for the women's movement. It allowed, in a conservative fashion, for women to belong to an organization with traditional and respected history, while giving them a voice. Morris had created a system of degrees that could be duplicated and passed on easily enough through ritual. The Order was established as an androgynous branch where both men and women were members and the timing was right for attracting women to a fraternity that was well respected and established in the Masonic lodges that were part of the villages and townships growing across the country.

Morris' enthusiasm for the Order of the Eastern Star was met with resistance by those who felt women had no place in masonry or anything else that gave women voice in business, government, or social structure. Dubbed by some as "Petticoat Masonry" Morris was threatened and cajoled and ridiculed. As Morris stated: "More than one writer in Masonic journals (men of an evil class, we have had them, men who know the secrets, but have never applied the principles of Masonry), more than one such expressed in language indecent and shocking, his opposition to me and the Eastern Star. Letters were written to me, some signed, some anonymous, warning me that I was periling my own Masonic connections in the advocacy of this scheme. In New York City the opponents of the Eastern Star even started a rival project to break it down. They employed a literary person, a poet of eminence, a gentleman of social merit, to prepare rituals under an ingenious form, and much time and money were spent in the effort to popularize it, but is survived only a short year and is already forgotten"(Kenaston, 1917, p. 22.)

When Morris began conferring "degrees" there was no large-scale plan that would allow the Order to expand. Morris tried to establish a Constellation of Families that would provide a framework for the Order to grow. He created the first Eastern Star Purity Constellation, No. 1 at Lodgeton, Ky. at the Union Church. Other constellations were created, but the constellation framework was unsuccessful. There was confusion over the framework and its organization making it difficult to initiate.

Morris made Jonathon Leonard in New York the agent for helping to establish the Constellations across the country. Unfortunately, Leonard was untrustworthy and accused of un-masonic like conduct. Morris began to change the operation of Constellations into Families and published *The Rosary of the Eastern Star* (1865) which helped to clarify ritual and meaning of the degrees and operations within the Order.

As the Civil War ended, Morris began to focus his attention on a trip to the Middle East to study the roots of freemasonry and establish a lodge in Jerusalem. In 1866, Morris endorsed his friend, Robert Macoy, to take over the organization of the Eastern Star, so Morris could raise funds for his trip

A marker at Smith Park in downtown Jackson, MS. The marker
is close to where the Morris's resided in Jackson.

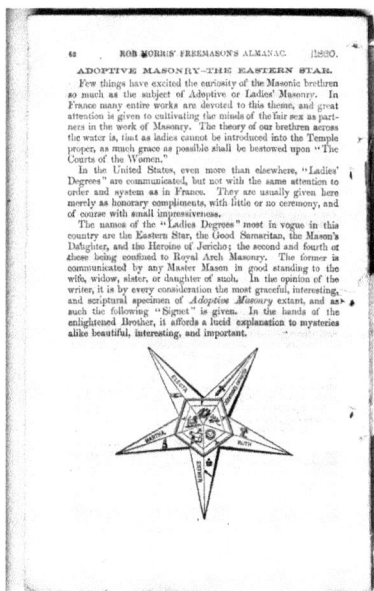

In Morris's "Freemason's Almanac" 1860 he presented a
"Signet" of the Adoptive Masonry—The Eastern Star.

The Union Church near Lodgeton Kentucky was the site of Purity
Lodge No. 1, the first chapter of the Order of the Eastern Star.

THE LADIES' MASONRY,
OR HIEROGLYPHIC MONITOR,

Containing all the emblems explained in the degrees of the Holy Virgin,
and Heroine of Jericho, duly arranged, by M. W. William Leigh, P. G.
M. G. L. Ala. To which are added Illustrations,

ADDRESSES, &C., FROM THE LOUISVILLE JOURNAL.—" Masonic—the
object of the author is to insure uniformity in conferring those degrees of
honor, to which all Worthy Master Masons, their Wives, Widows, Mothers,
Sisters and Daughters, are entitled; we are satisfied of its great utility
and importance to the Masonic World."

This book advertisement for "The Ladies' Masonry" appeared
in Rob Morris's book "Lights and Shadows of Freemasonry"
in 1852 during the very early years of the Eastern Star.

to the Holy Lands. The Family System began to fade out as Macoy's leadership helped to advance the organization's direction with a new system of hierarchal degrees that still exist today. But, the system still had flaws and it wasn't until 1874 when Rev. Willis D. Engle publicly proposed a Supreme Grand Chapter of Representatives from the several Grand Chapters and "a revision and general boiling down and finishing up of the ritual which is now defective both in style and language." Not content with saying this was a proper thing to do, Brother Engle vigorously started to work to bring about the conditions he believed to be most desirable. Delegates from the Grand Chapters of California, Illinois, Indiana, Missouri, and New Jersey, met in Indianapolis, November 15-16, 1876, on the invitation of the Grand Chapter of Indiana. Grand Patron James S. Nutt, of Indiana, welcomed the visitors and opened the meeting. Brother John M. Mayhew, of New Jersey, was elected President, and Brother John R Parson, of Missouri, Secretary. A constitution was adopted, a committee appointed on revision of the ritual, and a General Grand Chapter duly organized.

The second session of the General Grand Chapter was held in Chicago, May 8-10, 1878, and the name of the organization became officially The General Grand Chapter of the Order of the Eastern Star. The Most Worthy Grand Patron was then the executive head, though in later years this was decided to be the proper province of the Most Worthy Grand Matron.

For most Masonic endeavors throughout Morris' career, he barely eked out a living and the Eastern Star was no exception as he explained: "I may call to witness the thousand groups of men and women who, in all these years, have sat under my voice while communicating the instructions of the Eastern Star, that no greed of money has actuated me in this work. How often have I refused fees offered me! How forbidden collections to be made for my benefit! Monitors of the Eastern Star have been published by twenties of thousands, but the money profits were enjoyed by others, not me. It is with honest pride that I make, as I have so often made, these declarations" (Kenaston, 1917, p. 24.)

The First Era of the Order of the Eastern Star ended when Morris handed over the organization of the Eastern Star to Rob Macoy. It is very difficult to assess the impact of Morris' hard work that elevated the Order of the Eastern Star as a credible and important contribution to the women's movement in the United States and the world. It was the first organization in the United States that gave women a voice on a national scale. It provided a network from a local to national level where women were encouraged to meet and discuss issues that improved people's lives. This was an extraordinary accomplishment given the distance that separated the frontier communities from each other and the more metropolitan areas in the eastern United States. The OES gave women a platform of visibility at a time when women had little opportunity in business, government, and education. It stood as a beacon for women to get involved locally as well as nationally and internationally to improve society. It embodied the power of women as a force to make positive changes.

The Chapters of the Order of the Eastern Star now encircle the earth. There are 430,000 members belonging to 4,600 Chapters. The Grand Chapters exist in every continental state in the United States, all Canadian provinces and in Bolivia, Italy, Puerto Rico, and Sao Paulo (Brazil.) Subordinate Chapters under the direct supervision of the General Grand Chapter, exist in Alaska, Aruba, Brazil Columbia, Germany, Guam, Hawaii, Mexico, Peru, Philippines, Romania, and Taiwan.

The Grand Chapters of New York and New Jersey are independent of General Grand Chapter. Eastern Star also exists in other foreign countries through the supreme Grand Chapter of Scotland and the United Grand Chapter of Australia (also independent of General Grand Chapter.)

The last triennium (2009-2012) saw charitable funds totaling over $17 million raised by the members of Grand General Chapter for numerous philanthropies including Cancer, Heart, and educational scholarships, Eastern Star Training Awards for Religious Leadership, Service Dogs and youth development.

General Grand Chapter recognizes and supports four historical landmarks as a part of its outreach:

The International Eastern Star Headquarters in Washington, D.C. (formerly the Perry Belmont Mansion)

The Rob Morris Home in LaGrange, Ky.

The Little Red Schoolhouse in Richland, Ms.

The International Peace Garden Chapel on the border of North Dakota (US) and Manitoba (Canada).

CHAPTER EIGHT

Letters Between Rob and Son John

As the oldest son, John had the responsibility of taking care of the family in his father's absence. The initial letters from Rob to John were usually written as addendums to the letters to wife Charlotte. By 1852, John, age nine, began writing back to his father to bring him up to date on life at Lodgeton, Kentucky which gives a snapshot of the day-to-day activities of the Morris family. Morris created the Lodgeton Post Office because of his massive amount of correspondence in his work. "He was the 'Nasby,' contractor and mail-carrier" and the post office became the depository of the local mail: "and everything, without bar, bolt, or lock, was accessible to all comers and goers, with no more obstruction than the tumble-down rail fence, the rude door on its wooden hinges, and a mangy cur that warned against the approach of cowans and eavesdroppers as well as other more welcome visitors" (Rule, 1922, p. 26.) Charlotte's letters were much briefer, particularly in the latter part of the decade, as John took over the letter writing. In addition to carrying for the children, Charlotte was plagued with reoccurring bouts of chills and aches from yellow fever.

By the end of the decade, son Alfred had become a good writer and began his correspondences with Rob. When the family moved to Louisville, both Alfred and John were fully engrossed in their father's business, keeping track of shipping, and receiving records and all types of correspondence. The following letters span through the decade of the 1850s up until the family moved to LaGrange when Rob took a job as headmaster at the Kentucky Masonic College. They give depth to the context of the era and circumstances of the family's living conditions and Morris' activities across the country.

February 15, 1852 from Henryville, Tennessee

My Dear Son

I got your letter dated January 29 and right glad I was to hear that every thing was getting along so well. The hens are laying pretty fast to save twenty four eggs so quick as you did. I hope you will take care not to let the hens hide their nests so that you can't find them. I was delighted to hear that he cow had been driven home and was giving so much milk. Good sweet milk is the best thing that children can eat. It makes them healthier and fat. It is much better for them than coffee or tea.

I have bought you a bound volume of *Songs for the People* and shall bring it home when I come. You will be interested in the songs I am sure.

I cut out a pretty story called *Harry Lee's Temptation* and now send it to you. I couldn't help feeling sorry for poor Harry but then I felt so glad that it all came out right. Things always come out right when we do right for God see us and he loves those who do right.

From your affectionate Father

On Steamboat Columbian, June 20, 1852:

My dear John

I shall write something to you every Sunday and I will write it so plain that you can read it yourself.

I got on the S. B. Howard and came up the Ohio River as far as Paducah. Look on the map of the Western States and see where Paducah is. The S. B. Howard was going up the Cumberland river to Nashville and as I did not want to go up the Cumberland river to Nashville but I wanted to go up the Ohio river to Louisville I had to get off at Paducah and wait for a boat. So I got off and I took my heavy carpet bag in my hand and umbrella under my arm and walked up the hill to the hotel. No sooner did I sit down and beg to read a paper than I heard a puff, puff, puff. So I looked out and there was the Columbian. She had just come down the Tennessee river from Clifton with a load of iron and was going up the Ohio river past Evansville and past Owensborough and past Louisville and past Cincinnati clear to Pittsburg. So I got on the Columbian on Thursday night and I shall get to Louisville tonight. Look on the map for Tennessee river, Clifton, Cumberland river, Nashville, Evansville, Owensborough, Louisville, Cincinnati and Pittsburg. This is a very small boat.

It is a stern wheel boat. The Clerk on it is named Lyons. He is a Mason and he is a good man as all Masons ought to be. They do not keep any liquor to sell on this boat and nobody plays cards. They only made me pay six dollars from Paducah to Louisville.

Now my son take good care of my letters after you read them.

From your father Rob Morris

I send you some pens that Mr. Lyons gave me.

Rob and Charlotte's oldest son, John Anson Morris, born Sept. 17, 1843 at Oxford, MS. Courtesy of *The Grand Chapter of Kentucky, OES.*

Rob and Charlotte's son, Alfred Morris, born April 3, 1847. Courtesy of *The Grand Chapter of Kentucky, OES.*

Morris always carried his flute with him during his travels for his personal entertainment. Courtesy of *The Grand Chapter of Kentucky, OES.*

Rob and Charlotte's daughter, Charlotte Fales Morris, born May 12, 1845. Courtesy of *The Grand Chapter of Kentucky, OES.*

Louisville, July 4, 1852 (excerpt)

My Dear Son John

I am sitting in my bedroom in the third story . My room is number ten. I always lock it up when I go down stairs and leave the key with the clerk because there are wicked folks in this city who go round the hotels at night and if they find a room unlocked they go in and steal everything they can find. One night last week there was a thief found stealing things and they sent him to jail and he will have to stay there a good while, maybe three years or more.

Last Monday they tolled all the bells and then I found that Mr. Clay, that great man was dead. He died in Washington City about eleven o'clock and we heard it here in two hours afterwards. Everybody was sorry because Mr. Clay was a great man and he lived in Kentucky and everybody loved him. Next Friday they will bring his body home in a coffin and everybody will go to the steamboat and look at the coffin. And the steamboat will be all dressed in black with flags. And the cannons will be fired and the bells will ring again.

Last Thursday the stores were shut up and the schools turned out the whole day because everybody was so sorry that Mr. Clay is dead. Henry Clay was a great man, a wise man. Before he died he said he was willing to die because he believed that God had pardoned all his sins and he thought he should go to heaven. I hope he has gone to heaven and that all my children will go there too and that ma and pa will go there too. I would rather that all my children should die now than not to go to heaven.

I went to Sunday school this morning. There was a hundred boys and girls. But I don't think they studied much and they would not sing any and they did not behave well. There was a blind man there who can walk all over the city without anybody to lead him and he never gets lost. He makes brushes, that is his business and he can make mighty good brushes if he is blind.

I went to church this morning and heard a good sermon. This is the fourth of July, Independence Day. If it was not Sunday there would be a great celebration today. American people should never forget the fourth of July for that was the day when our forefathers periled their lives for freedom's sake and thousands of them were killed.

From your dear father.

Newcastle, Kentucky, July 25, 1852 (excerpt)

My dear John

When I read your little letter to me I said to my self that is the first letter I ever got from one of my children and the boy who wrote it shall have a drum. So I went to a music store where they sell all sorts of musical things and I picked out a drum, a real splendid drum. Now it was none of your cheap drums, no sir. It cost most two dollars and is just as good a drum as the drums that soldiers use ...

They had a great temperance meeting here last week. There were five hundred persons on the ground. I came here on the railroad which runs from Louisville. You must look for that railroad on the map and in Henry County you will see this town Newcastle. It is quite a pretty place and nobody keeps any whiskey to sell so there are no drunken people.

Last Sunday some boys went in swimming in the river at Louisville and one of them got into a deep place and sunk to the bottom and was drowned. His poor mother how bad she felt. But she ought to have told him to keep Sunday better than that. This is from your affectionate father.

Louisville, Sept. 21, 1852 (excerpt)

My Dear little boy

We have got a cat in the printing office named Tom. He stays all day and sleeps around among the piles of papers and when night comes catches mice. I sleep in the printing office now. I bought a cot bed and mattress, sheets, blanket and everything and when bedtime comes, all I have to do is just to roll in and go to sleep. But when I wake up in the night, the room is so lonesome that it make me quite homesick.

Louisville, December 24, 1852 (excerpt)

Dear John and Charlotte

I want you to take care of your caps and boots and shoes and clothes. Don't' burn them nor lose them nor tear them. Make them last as long as you can for it takes a heap of money to keep you all in such things.

I ate some bear meat for breakfast this morning, and it was just as fat as a goose. I reckon the bear would rather have staid in the woods and eat hogs. Two numbers of *The Faithful Slave* have come and I shall get another tomorrow. It will be in a book and I will get one. It has eight pictures.

Last Sunday while I was at church just as the preacher had begun his sermon there was a cry of fire and everybody ran out. A great many houses were burnt close behind the church but God saved the church.

Louisville, Jan 23, 1853 (excerpt)

Dear John

The Faithful Slave is all printed now- all but one chapter. Soon as that comes from Boston I am going to send the whole piece to you. Mr. Robinson wrote to me lately that he will be here next week. But he won't find his umbrella here and I don't believe he will ever get it again unless you send it to him in a letter.

Do you remember Old Judge Hutchinson who lived in Jackson? He is dead. I can tell you an interesting story about him when I get home, how he was taken prisoner and put in jail for twelve months.

There is a cat stays in this printing office all the time. We call him Tom. The printers bring him bits of cold meat from their boarding houses and Tom is very sociable. I got a letter from Robert McKay last week. Do you remember him?. .

One of the biggest hotels in this city caught fire a few days ago and burnt a good deal. As soon as it got on fire a whole crowd of men and boys ran in and began to steal everything they could lay their hands on. Fourteen of them were caught and put in jail.

Write long letters to me every week.

From your father

Litchfield, Kentucky, December 25, 1853 (excerpt)

My Dear son John

The Cumberland Presbyterians have a church here and last Sunday they got me to preach twice for them. It is only twenty miles from here to the great Mammoth Cave, the greatest Cave in the world. That cave runs ten miles under ground. I have a story to tell Sis about some ladies that went into that cave and like to have got drowned. I rode my poney Phil about twenty miles on Friday. He is the greatest little poney every you saw. He trots so easy. And he will go to mill or plow or go in a little wagon or let you and Alfred ride on his back. I hope I can bring him home with me and leave him there and then he shall belong to my boys. He don't like a switch much but I just lay it to him and Mr. Morehead lays a spur and jab to him when he gets a little lazy. Is our cistern dug? Is the garden plowed? Is the chimney finished? I will be along there in a few weeks and see.

From your Father.

April the 12, 1854 (excerpt)

My Dear Pa

I am glad to inform you that we are all well and doing well. I have learned to play on the accordion without making one mistake in most every song. I can play "Hunters of Kentucky" and a good man others. I have not hurt it in any way yet. I don't let no body have it but Mrs. Calvert and a few others who comes here. We went to Mr. and Mrs. Donals and stayed a week down there- me and Henry found birds nests and got some, plowed up some young rabbits but the plow killed them. It is Spring here now and everything is green, the woods so green and pretty. Ma has not got nothing planted but few Irish potatoes but we will plant more before long. You must make hast and come home for it is time to go a fishing. I went a fishing the other day and caught one but that was not a last for us ...

From your son John Morris

Lodge, Kentucky, August 8, 1856 (excerpt)

My Dear Father

We are all well at present and I hope these few lines will find you enjoying the same blessing. Our school is out and there is not any school now and their will not be any more before a good while. I helped at the mill last week but I did not stay there today. They are a grinding corn now and will grind as long as they can get corn to grind. We have go 100 bundles of fodder saved and if the weather is good we can save as many more. It has been a raining so far the last week that Alfred could not do much at it but he pulled some and tied up what he had pulled the front field is gathered from the side next the new stables below the corn cribs. Ma got you letter from New

York today after Peckham went to Hickman today and will be back to night or to morrow one.

There is a good many sick persons around here now. Mrs. Williams is dead and Mr. Ropers children died last week. Mrs. Boyd and Mrs. Cos are both sick but they both are getting better. Mrs. Brown's folks have been sick but are al a getting well.

The mill will be a grinding wheat in a month or so they have got the new main shaft in and both engines a minning the meal comes out every near as fast as they can take it up. It is hot wen it comes out. Everybody is a bringing in corn to have ti ground up into meal. They commenced a grinding Friday. It ground a bushel in two minutes and twelve bushels in a half an hour.

From you affectionate son John A. Morris

Cleveland Ohio, April 26, 1857

Mr. John A. Morris, Lodgeton, Kentucky

My Dear Sir

I have the honor to pay you my respects and hope that they will be cordially reciprocated. Since I took you by the parting hand I have journeyed via Louisville, Cincinnati and Columbus to this place and

...

You see, my Boy, how rigid and stiff that sort of letter is.That is the way business men begin their letters, cold and formal and as dull as a Barlow knife. But you and I don't use that syle. We prefer the affectionate style. We love to tell each other how great is our affection how strong is our attachment, how ardent is our love, how lasting is our friendship.

This morning before breakfast I walked to the edge of the bluff on which this city is situated and looked out over the Lake towards Canada. The water was quiet as a pool. Far in the East the long trail of black smoke showed where some steamer was just descending beneath the horizon. Not a vessel was stirring. Flags and sails drooped in the total quietude of the morning. It was indeed a calm and fitting scene for a Sabbath morning.

My Dear Boy, I depend greatly upon you to assist your mother. She is now in a condition that she cannot bear noise and irritation. Any quarrel or cavil among the children will distress her more than you can imagine until you get older. Be kind and gentle to your dear

Mother who has never spared any pains or trouble to make you happy. How often have I seen her the whole night long bending over you when you were sick and she never complained. Cannot you then be affectionate to her? Spare no sacrifices to save her trouble and as all you can to help her. Be a guide and example to Alfred and Robert. They will shape this course pretty much by you. Look around the place every evening as you return from school and see that nothing is lost, mislaid or wasted.

I am delighted to see how dearly you love good books. Nothing better serves to keep boys from evil courses than a literary taste. Write up you diary every day without fail. How much I shall enjoy to read it when I come home. Mention every little incident that occurs day by day. Mention the height of the thermometer, the changes of the weather, the incidents of the school, the little affairs of the neighborhood, everything that I will want to know when I get home.

God bless you , my dear son. You and I have had many happy hours together. I believe there is nothing you love better than to make me happy. Try to honor and obey your Mother and remember the Fifth Commandment.

From your affectionate Father

Montreal Canada, May 17, 1857

Dear Son John

On Thursday I sailed from Toronto to this place on the Steamer Kingston. Look at the map and you will see that I came down Lake Ontario and then down the River St. Lawrence. When I get home be sure to ask me about the Thousand Islands and the Rapids and the Indian pilot who came on board in a canoe to pilot us over the most dangerous rapids that ever I saw. The Rapids under the suspension bridge are nothing to them.

Oh how sick I was on Lake Ontario. I vomited everything that I had eat for two days. And the confounded sailor only laughed at me- one of them had the cruelty to advise me to drink some gin! Enough! The boat was an iron boat, the first one I ever sailed in.

There is a British Regiment stationed here and the Red Coats can be met in every street. It is the 17th Regiment, one of those that was so badly cut up before Sebastopol. Many of them wear the medals given them for their bravery in that war. But people say here that they are sad, drunkards and blackguards and no decent folks associate with them. Somehow when I meet one I cannot help thinking of Bunker Hill and how their scarlet coats were spread over the earth after that desperate array. The great Tubular Bridge over the St. Lawrence is here. It will take five years to finish it and will cost six millions of dollars. It will be the greatest and most costly bridge I believe in the world. It is for the cars to pass over.

A steamship sailed from here yesterday night to Liverpool, so you see they have a connection direct with the mother country. There is an immense business done between Canada and Great Britain. It was here that Tom Moore wrote those beautiful lines,—" Faintly as tolls the evening chime, Our voices keep tune and our oars keep time"

This place was taken by General Arnold in the Revolutionary War. By the time I write to you again I shall be able to tell you something about Quebec where Wolfe was killed and where Montgomery was afterwards killed.

Get ma to read you a part of my letter to her or let you read all of it if she chooses.

Goodnight my loving son, Pray, your father.

Burlington, Vermont May 31, 1857 (excerpt)

Dear John

Right where I sit is the scene of the great fight on sea and land where McDonough took the British fleet. I saw the place where his ships were built at Vergennes. They came down the Lake Champlain past the place and fought the British at Plattsburg in sight of here. I shall have a large number of stories to tell that have been told me her by the people who were in the fight and by others who saw it. Don't forget to ask me for the anecdote of McDonough stabbing three of his own sailors.

Since I wrote to you I have stood where Wolfe was killed on the plains of Abraham at Quebec. Where General Montgomery was killed, where the strongest fort is that is in America. I shall have much to tell you about Quebec. My visit to the great Citadel there was a curious thing. I got up on one of the cannons to look over the wall but the sentinel put me off of that in a hurry. They don't allow anybody to do that. I saw the 16th Regiment of the British make a fine review in the Plains of Abraham. It was a grand sight. They moved together like one man though, there were 500 of them .They loaded, fired, advanced, retreated, like one man. Their deep red coats and shining guns and sharp bayonets make a splendid appearance.

I have got some of the shot that was captured from the British by McDonough also a sheet of cartridge paper for loading a cannon, and I shall bring them home for you museum. A ship captain at Quebec also presented me with a Chinese idol very curious which I shall bring home ...

Philadelphia, July 25, 1857 (excerpt)

Dear John

Here I am in this city of William Penn styled "the City of Brotherly Love." The word Philadelphia means "a house of Brothers" and was so named by that old Quaker William Penn to commemorate his own friendly principles and to teach those who should hereafter settle here what kind of spirit ought to animate them in their intercourse with one another. So kindly did Penn treat the Indians that while almost every other white settlement was engaged in constant wars with the Indian tribes, for seventy years Penn's settlement were at peace. No doubt peace is the safest and best for everybody.

Diary entries from John written from Lodgeton, Ky.

August 5, 1857

Today has been a very hot day in doors and out doors for there was not much a stirring and what their was stirring it was so warm that it made it worse than if it had not been. I have been hauling oats all this evening we got half done and put them up over the corn. Mr. Breast went to Hickman yesterday and will not be back till tomorrow evening. I have been sick nearly all day although I did help to haul up the oats. I have got risings in both of my ears and they ach nearly all the time so that I could not finish my diary.

August 6

Today was not as hot as yesterday was. We finished hauling oats this evening . We did not get to work till after dinner. We hauled one load before dinner but it was a big load. Alfred had to go to Mr. Wm. Brown's to help put in some resin to his well. The mill ran most all night last night grinding wheat.They run the mill regular now in the day time but they have not got wood hauled up to run it every night. It keeps one wagon hauling all the time. My ears are no better today. I have had a fever all day very near.

Saturday, August 8

Today was a tolerable clear day nearly all day. It was a little cloudy what dinner time. But is didn't rain any. We have been shucking corn nearly all day. I don't know when we are a going to shell it the mill has been running all day grinding wheat. They have got the wheat piled up in the mill so that you cannot hardly get about in it for the wheat. I didn't think that there could be so much wheat collect out one place.

Sunday August 9

Today has been a pretty day as good as we might expect. I went to Sunday School this morning and said a lesson in the question book and read the fourth chapter of Mathew an our lesson next Sunday is a page and a half in the question book and the fifth, sixth and seventh chapter of Mathew to read and it will be a long lesson. There was black folks meeting there again today and there was a good many of them caught playing cards and drinking liquor.

Monday, August 10

Today has been a day long to be remembered for the rain that fell today it rained till dinner time and put the creeks out of their banks everywhere. I never saw it rain so hard before in my life. You could not see no ways before you for the rain it cleared off about dinner time. But you could not get about much for the water the yard looked like a river while it was raining but it all soon sun down in the creeks. The mill is still a going it like it bust but its best chance to run and trying to make up for it.

Lodge, Kentucky, August 11, 1857 (excerpt)

My Dear Father

We are all well and hope that you are enjoying the same. The weather is very wet now not withstanding. Our corn looks well as any bodies corn but it has not got awasting corn on it yet. I got three big one the other day is all that has been got out of there yet. Me and Alfred Lewis have hauled up the oats we borrowed Mr. Brown's wagon and oxen to haul them up. We put part of them over the corn but we left a place to throw in the corn this fall and a part of them over the passage and the rest over the stable. We have turned the cows in the oats field they don't' seem to disturb the apple trees. It looks like they ought to be turned in the wheat fields but Mr. Craig says he is a going to sell that pasture. He has sold ten barrels of our corn at a dollar and a half a bushel. He is a going to have it ground up.

Mr. Habunk went after the horses but he did not get them nor could not hear a word from them. All Pud ought to write a letter such home to us and let us know how he is and what sort of a place he has got to. Mr. Cincey has bought the longest pile of wheats I ever seen. He has got the mill all full just room enough for the machinery and a path to walk about in and he is filling up the old stone house with wheat. He runs the mill night and day just as hard as he can. One of his negroes run a way and he has not caught him yet. He offers 150 dollars for him dead or alive and there is a good many men after him.

Diary entries from John at Lodgeton, Ky.

Tuesday, August 18, 1857

Mr. Calvert found the horses and brought the grey mare home on Friday but he left Pud up there till he could get back and get him.

Friday, August 21st, 1857

Alfred has been shelling corn all day till a while after dinner. He had to go and help load some wagons with wheat over at the orchards to haul to Hickman to be shipped to New Orleans. Mr. Cincey didn't buy it.

Saturday, Aug. 22

It is so cold that we cannot do without a fire. I am beginning to think that it is most time we were getting ready our sleighs and have a sleigh ride. Mr. John Milner's daughter died today. She has been sick more than a year.

Sunday, Aug. 23

The sun shone out hot towards noon so that I thought hot weather was coming again but I was in hopes that It was not. I never went to Sunday School today for there was a burying at the grave yard and they broke up Sunday School for the scholars to go to the burying. It clouded up this evening and shone like it was a going to rain but it did not. There was a meeting at Rock Spring meeting house and a good many people left the graveyard and went there to hear them preach and drink whiskey. For they say that you can step out in the bushes and find a negro with a bottle of whiskey.

Wednesday, August 26

It has rained steady all day although not very hard but hard enough to keeping anybody in the house confined. We have been shelling corn this evening. We shelled about six bushels and we have been shucking corn the rest of the evening to shell tomorrow. We are going to finish the ten barrels.

Saturday, August 29, 1857

It has been a very pretty day although some too cold in the mornings and evening. I have been to Mr. Morgan's this morning to help make some cider and I drank a good deal, you may be sure. I went to the grave yard and help dig a grave for Mr. Brown of Clinton, one of Robert Brown's daughters, she is going to be buried tomorrow. There was a woman buried there last Sunday and there is a going to be one tomorrow.

Sunday, August 30

Today was a very good day for it seems like every body is trying to do good and the weather corresponds. I went to Sunday School but there was not any one on account of the burying but the corpse did not come til twelve o'clock. The Templars marched today but they did not seem to have any order about them if they had marched regular it would of looked well but it didn't look much. Mr. Ward preached her funeral. She was born in 1811.

Friday, Sept. 4th

The mill is still a going. It has not stopped more only on Sundays since Pa left. Alfred Lewis went to help work the road today. Ma had another chill but it was not very hard one and she soon got over it. Everybody almost has begun to gather fodder and we will begin soon if the weather keeps good.

Thursday, Sept. 10, 1857

A cloudy but hot day has past—it was the warmest day I ever seen to be cloudy. I helped shell corn this morning and pulled fodder this evening for myself I was to pull about five hundred bundles but I did not work long. Then boys went a fishing today but they didn't catch much.

Thursday, Sept. 17, 1857

It has been a pretty day. There was quite a noise up in town for a while this morning. One negro man stuck an ax with another one. It didn't kill him right off but I expect he will not live long. They both belongs to Mr. Milner and Mr. Cayce had them hired and I believe they fell out over some fodder. Mr. Cayce told them not to pull fodder every night and one of them did and the other one told on him and so he too his revenge.

New York City, September 21, 1857(excerpt)

My Dear John

Since I wrote to you the awful news has reached here of the total loss of the "Central America", a California steamer foundered at sea. It is fearful to think of more than 500 person drowned. But all the women and children are save that was one great blessing. All the heavy mails with 12000 letters and more than a million dollars in gold is lost. There has never before been a disaster with so large a number of person lost as this. I mean by the sinking of a steamer. Many a family is overwhelmed with distress by this accident and many a person has lost all he was worth ...

Your Father

Montgomery Alabama, Dec. 13, 1857(excerpt)

My Dear John

Two week have gone since we parted and this afternoon I shall turn my face northward and go by way of Marietta, Chattanooga and

Stevenson to Nashville, then by stage to Elizabethtown, Ky., there take the train to Louisville. It will be about four days very severe travel.

I suppose you have made considerable progress in that list of lodges by this time. The Grand Lodge of Alabama has agreed to pay for a set of the *Universal Masonic Library* for every lodge in this state. By your catalogue you can tell in a minute how many there are. I make it about 225. I know one thing, it is a big lot of books, nearly 7000 volumes.

I would suggest to you the propriety of what is called alternation of labor—that is to change frequently from one thing to another. The old philosophers used to say that a change of labor is equal to play. I have always found it so and therefore I recommend it to you. Write, for instance, an hour on that Indiana Lodge Record at Kaskaskia. Then work an hour on the Lodge Catalogue. Then work an hour pasting letters in the clip book. By this means you will never become much fatigued. Try it ...

Pensacola, Florida, January 31, 1858 (excerpt)

My Dear Son John

Last Sunday you know I was at Quincy.On Tuesday I went to Tallahassee and on Thursday to St. Marks. There is an old Spanish fort at St. Marks which is quite a curiosity. It was built about 100 years ago to repress the Indians. It is situated right in the fork of two rivers and the great, strong wall runs across form river to river with a deep ditch in front of it. It is now all in ruins however and the government is pulling it to pieces to build a hospital for sick sailors close by. Around St. Marks is abundance of the palmetto tree, the oddest looking tree I ever saw. I scarcely know how to describe it.

At that place there is one of the finest fishing grounds in the world. There they catch the sea bass, trout, sheepshead, grouper, perch, pompano, snapper and any quantity of turtles to oysters. The first think I did after arrival was to call for a large plate of raw oysters and it was truly wonderful to see the facility with which I devoured them. The river bed is buried with oysters they are so abundant I never saw a place I should so well like to bring you three boys to spend a week and fish as at St. Marks. But such hurricanes as they do have here. A few years ago there was a little town a few miles from there which blew entirely away and was never attempted to be rebuilt.

On Friday I took the steamer Atlantic for New Orleans. To my surprise I found on board a party of United States officers and some of the sailors of the United States ship of war "Wabash" and who do you think they had in charge for prisoners? Why no other than Colonel Anderson and 46 of his men whom they had captured in Nicaragua and were taking as prisoners to New Orleans.

If you have read the account of the capture of that party you will understand it. First General Walker was taken prisoner with all hi men by the "Saratoga" and carried to New York. A few weeks afterwards Colonel Anderson was captured and this is the last of the filibusters. When they get to New Orleans they shall be put in prison and tried but they don't seem to care for that. The officers play cards and smoke all the time. But many of them are sick and all of them look ragged and pitiable. It is sad to see so many young men engaged in such a miserable business.

The Gulf has been quite smooth and I have not been sick, only a little greenish. Yesterday we stopped at Apalachicola all day and today we spend here at Pensacola. Tomorrow afternoon we expect to get to New Orleans where I shall mail this letter. I am afraid the Gulf is going to be rough tonight as I see the waves look white out beyond the bar. The sea gulls are swooping around us and occasionally plunging down to the water after a fish and the scene is very animated ... there is a lot of tremendous great turtles on board going to New Orleans to be made into soup. They were brought from the Key West where turtles are very large and plenty! They lie quietly on their back waiting very patiently for whatever happens. I am afraid if we should get shipwrecked they would be glad of it so they could go to the bottom ...

Lodgeton, Kentucky, April 10, 1868 (excerpt)

My Dear Father

We could not haul wood today one of the oxen has been foundered up at the mill and he cannot more than walk let alone pull anything but I worked in the garden a part of the day. Lodgeton has got to be a right respectable looking place. They have got a new set of goods and the store barn and mill are crowded all the time except Sunday. There is a good deal of scarlet fever now about. Mr. Kimbro that lives at Rock Spring has lost two of his children by it and there is some more that is not expected to live ...

John S. Morris, Lodge, KY

Lodgeton, Kentucky, April 17th 1858 (excerpt)

My Dear Father

The family is all well at present although ma has had the chills this week she missed her chill day before yesterday and did not have one today. The neighborhood has got clear of the scarlet fever once more I believe. Mr. Kimbro lost all of his children with it. Mr. Wad is dead. I do not know what was the matter with him. He did not leave any will and they have appointed Mr. Craig his administrator and he is going to sell all the property.

Lodge, Kentucky, May 8, 1858 (excerpt)

My Dear Father

There is a good deal of sickness around here they have not got over the scarlet fever yet it is raging down on the state line, Mr. Cayce has just got it going about he has had the yellow jaundice and he looks like he had the yellow fever.

There has been school all this week. I went half of every day but Friday I went to Hickman. ... That box of books that was in Hickman has been brought out I opened it and took the books out and put them on the shelf for fear the mice would get in them. They are getting so bad I am afraid that they will commence on your books if they do I will take them down and put them in one of these big boxes and nail it up if there were to commence on them they would soon ruin a few of them ...

from your son J. A. Morris

CHAPTER NINE

The Masonic College of Kentucky

Prior to the founding of the new Republic of the United States in 1776, institutions of learning were established by the churches and under its control. Schools in the City of New York and elsewhere were either "pay schools" or purely sectarian in character, usually both. General Morgan Lewis, a well-known Mason, signer of the Declaration of Independence and speaker at George Washington's inauguration said:

> In a Government resting upon public opinion, and de-
> riving its chief support from the affections of the people,
> religion and morality cannot be too sedulously inculcat-
> ed. To these, science is a handmaid, ignorance the worst
> of enemies. Literary information should be placed with-
> in the reach of every description of citizens, and poverty
> should not be permitted to obstruct the path to the fane
> of knowledge. Common schools, under the guidance of
> respectable teachers, should be established in every vil-
> lage, and the indigent educated at the public expense. The
> higher seminaries also should receive every support and
> patronage within the means of enlightened legislators.
> Learning would thus flourish and vice be more effectually
> restrained, than by volumes of penal statutes (Pond, 1950,
> pp. 95–96.)

In the new democracy of the United States, education was not to be restricted to the privileged but an opportunity for all citizens. Masons, such
as George Washington and Benjamin Franklin, became founders of free
public schools. As people moved west, initiatives for education were strong.
Academies were initially formed in isolated communities where families
came together to pay instructor salaries. Masonic academies were con-
structed and offered higher levels of degrees for students. The academies
were often coed and included residences for students who often attended
from out of state. These academies were particularly popular in southern
communities that were more rural and had fewer advantages for educational opportunities than the more populated northeastern states.

A model of a Masonic college was created in LaGrange, Kentucky when
the Funk Seminary, which had been established through a donation by

William Funk in 1841, was transferred to the Grand Lodge in 1844. The school was managed by the Grand Lodge to be established "and endowed at the expense of the Grand Lodge and at which they might educate the orphans of Masonry on the labor principle by teaching them to practice healthy labor and mechanical arts in addition to the useful branches and English education." Citizens of LaGrange and Oldham County would be permitted to send their sons as "pay students" with tuition being $6 for primary students and $10 for Higher Department (Oldham County Historical Society, n.d.)

By 1847, females were also admitted to the College that created an enrollment in excess of 170 students (including charity students from 12 Lodges). The name of the institution was changed to The Masonic Seminary and Kentucky Masonic College. Through the diligent efforts of the Grand Lodge of Kentucky, the state legislature in 1850 deemed it appropriate to confer upon the college the full rights and privileges of a university. It was at this time that the name was changed again to The Masonic University of Kentucky. In this year, the Grand Lodge of Kentucky appropriated $1,000 for the education of female children of deceased Master Masons (Ibid.)

From 1850 to 1861, the Masonic University of Kentucky was very popular with full enrollment and a reputation for excellent scholarship. Reports from records at the Ky. Grand Lodge in 1845 show an enrollment of 203 students, 41 from Louisiana, 17 from Mississippi, with a representation of students from nine different states. The catalogue of the institution during these years proves its rank with Centre College and Transylvania University in the make-up of the faculty and the number and progress of the pupils (Ibid.)

Rob Morris was well aware of the educational initiatives that were taking place in Kentucky when he was living in Mississippi and encouraged those efforts to be emulated at places like the Eureka Masonic College at Richland, Mississippi. Morris' move to Louisville in 1860 with his family put him in close vicinity to LaGrange and it was logical that he was recruited as a faculty member to teach ancient history. Under state law, The Masonic University of Kentucky was granted the right to confer the title of LL.D, a doctor of law degree, which they conferred to Morris in 1860. From thence forward, Rob Morris was Dr. Rob Morris, LL.D. and began to include that title in all his correspondence and publications (Rule, 1922, p. 87.)

In circulars sent to lodges across the South, LaGrange was described as a "beautiful, thriving town, the county seat of Oldham County, convenient

The Masonic University of Kentucky in LaGrange was established in 1852 reaching peak attendance shortly before the Civil War. Courtesy of *The Oldham County Historical Society.*

After the Civil War the Masonic University reverted to a local school until it burned in 1911. State marker located on First and Jefferson Streets in LaGrange, KY.

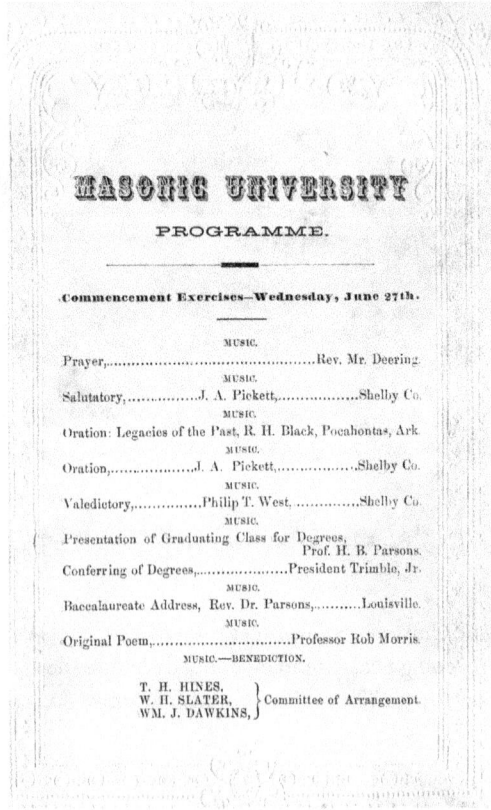

A program depicting commencement exercises in 1862 for the Masonic
University of Kentucky. *Courtesy of Oldham County Historical Society.*

This brick home was built by surveyor William Barbour and later became
a girl's dormitory for the Masonic University of Kentucky in LaGrange.

Part of the attraction for the Masonic College in LaGrange was access to the railroad which still operates through the center of the town.

ROB MORRIS HOME, LaGrange, Ky.

The Rob Morris home site late 1800s when porch and balcony were attached. Morris's office was located off the balcony. *Courtesy of Oldham County Historical Society.*

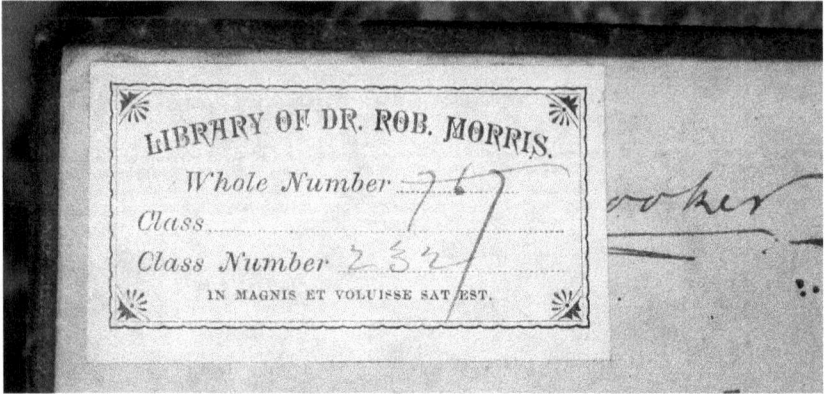

Morris had an extensive book collection in his library, some of which burned in his first home, located in LaGrange called The Apricot. He was able to rebuild his collection. This bookmark indicates book number 767.

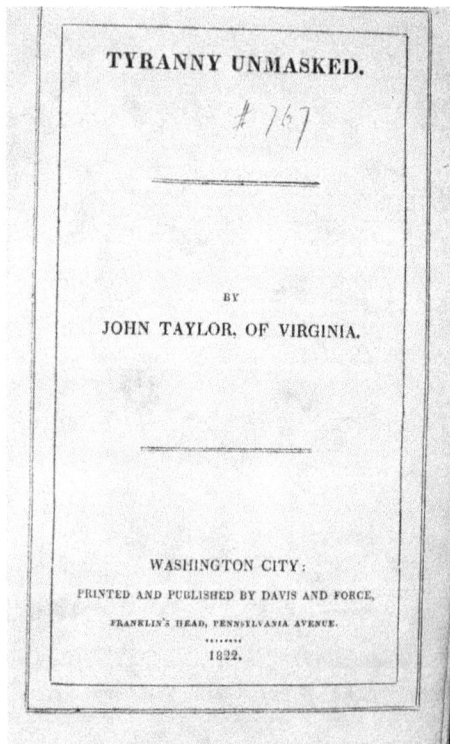

One of Morris's rare books in his collection, Book 767,
Tyranny Unmasked by John Taylor, 1822.

to Louisville, the Ohio River, Shelbyville and Newcastle. The situation is high and healthy and the citizens sober, intelligent and industrious, with not a grog shop in town" (Oldham County Historical Society, n.d.)

The Morris family finally found a permanent home in LaGrange; The bustling railroad town had four hotels nestled by the railroad tracks, numerous restaurants, and plenty of local shops whose shelves were regularly re-stocked with items supplied daily by the trains. The town was truly a railroad town with rail tracks placed on the Main Street allowing trains to travel directly through all the stores and shops on each side of the street. Located 29 miles northeast of Louisville, LaGrange was a summer getaway for many who wanted to escape the heat and mosquitoes from the nearby river city.

Morris had an extensive reference library of books he collected from his vast travels. Unfortunately, many of the books were lost in a house fire causing the Morris family to move to a new home on Washington Street which is now a shrine and preserved by the Kentucky Grand Chapter of OES.

Each day, a sack full of letters arrived at the Morris household among the activities of teenage children and their beloved dog, Leo, a large shepherd mix who was said to accompany Morris on his walks through the town. Morris worked dutifully at his desk each day as well as prepared his weekly seminar on Ancient History for the students at the Ky. Masonic College.

The following letter was written by Salem Towne in November, 1860, when he visited Morris. Salem Towne was Grand Chaplain of New York.

> *His domicile I found at LaGrange, Ky., twenty-nine miles out of Louisville on the Frankfort railroad. I assed through a fertile and nice region to reach it, but the little town lacks houses and people to make it as large as Jeddo and a man might go through the place without knowing it. The landlord of the inn pointed me to a neat two-story building on the edge of the village as the whereabouts of 'Dr. Morris' as he styled him. I passed a neat green park which surrounds the county court house. Then the "Three Cedars" loomed up before me, from which Bro. Morris' place is named, slips from which cedars are found in the portfolios of his friends far and near. Entering the gate I was at once in the presence.*
>
> *Bro. Morris is exactly a fathom in height, straight as a Pawnee Loup, and supple as a cat. His hand-grip is like a vise, and he has a way of his own of catching a fellow by the right shoulder when he is really glad to*

see him. I saw him do it several times to his visitors while I was there, and learned to discriminate by that mark their character. His voice is deep, swift, and pleasant as music to the ear. He had me down by his side, or rather tete-a-tete within thirty seconds, and I was at home in thirty more.

His Sanctum Sanctorum is a small hall-room in the second story of his dwelling, and not more than 18x12 feet in dimensions. What with the three desks, shelving for books, piles of 'copy boxes,' letter boxes, miscellaneous boxes, chairs, and great folios and quartos too huge for earthly shelves to hold, he is elegantly crowded. But he likes that. He says he wants everything at his hand from a 'Morgan to an Oliver', judging by appearances, he has it.

And first, his library. This consists of about 1,200 bound volumes, most of them made up of tracts and pamphlets of small size upon every conceivable theme of Masonry and Anti-Masonry. Of course there is an index, itself an immense folio, which catalogues each work by author and subject, but, as he confesses, this is quite imperfect as to what it should be. Nearly every volume in this collection has its history. Some are presents from the dead, some from the living. Some were procured in Maine; some in Texas. Some were esteemed of the least possible value b their former owners. A considerable number were gleanings of that active individual, Bro. E.D. Cooke, in Western New York and Europe. Amongst the former he shows works presented him by Bros. Mix. Reynolds, Brown, Chesebro, Whitney, Gould, Towne, and others; amongst the latter valuable presents from Dr. Oliver, Dr. Ladd, Bros. Warren, Wilson, etc. England, Scotland and Ireland. A hasty estimate of these pieces collected here, counting portraits and medals, as well as printed pieces, makes the amount to exceed fifty thousand, yet the greedy fellow speaks slightly of his acquisitions in this line; complains that many to whom he writes begging letters on this subject do not respond, and earnestly solicited me, when I should return to collect up and send him anything from a copy of by-laws to a bound folio in one hundred volumes!

To say that it is strange how Bro. Morris gets through the labor he does poorly expresses the fact; it is wonderful, marvelous, miraculous. The day I was with him, though he was talking to me nearly all ; the time, and listening to me when his tongue was still, he wrote and posted twenty-nine letters (I counted them myself); wrote a circular relative to his paper (The Voice);overhauled corrected and prepared for publication a considerable pile f copy for the Voice and wrote at least one or two column articles as a leader. And when I asked him if he was not trying himself he smiled *grimly and said, "That was no day's work at all." I never saw a man get over work so rapidly. For instance, his mail brought him sixteen letters; a single glance at each revealed their contents, and to reply to the whole did not occupy him an hour. His partner at Louisville sends out every night the correspondence of the day, all of which h reads, and replies to such as embrace questions of Masonic law, etc., which a considerable part do. He showed me his list of private and confidential correspondents. This embraces nearly every well-known leader of the Masonic Craft, and with these he corresponds monthly. But his general correspondents county by thousands, and the subjects are innumerable as the sands on the sea shore.*

I regretted that it was vacation in the University as I had heard many favorable things concerning it, its President and faculty. Of the latter Bro. Morris is Professor of History (Ancient and Modern) and gives a lecture every Friday evening. I was glad to hear that shortly before my arrival the Board of Trustees of the University had honored him and two other distinguished Masons, whose names I have lost, with the merited honor of LL.D.

But to see him work! Right above him the portrait of John Fitz Towsend, Grand Master of Ireland. At a desk on his right his oldest son, a promising youth of eighteen, whose labors, he says are invaluable; behind him (working as little as possible folding and copying) his other two lads. The mocking birds upon the locust tree on the lawn; the three cedars, rich in their verdancy, below the window; the cooing of pigeons, the barking of- ah, big Leo, I pardon your honest nip, in view of your after repentance and scratch, scratch, scratch, with an old fashioned quill pen (bought by half hundred ready made), the great missionary of the Craft! It was a sight to remember as long as memory abides faithful.

The eyesight of my illustrious host is fast becoming enfeebled and he has been compelled, for the most pat, to interdict candle light reading and writing; therefore when night came, he turned away to four charming little girls, who claimed his knees and clamored for his kisses, and taking me down in a broad beautiful park nearby gave me, until long past low XII, a sketch of his labors, trials and hopes. I found him very sensitive on the score of personal abuse. To be stabbed at through the press, and by such men as his assaulters- men vulnerable at every opening; to be accused of mercenary dealings; when he entailed nothing but poverty upon himself and family in reward of all his Masonic labors, he acknowledges to suffer more pain from these sources than all his business troubles and ill health united.

> *But when he speaks of the future; when he opens out the plan of his life, and descants upon the glorious results to follow upon the success of the enterprises in which he is embarked; where he describes the great Craft all speaking with one tongue, and doing one work, and pursuing one aim and seeking one reward, the pale face lightens up, the eye beams with generous fire, and the inner man is fully developed. No man can say he knows Rob Morris until he has caught him in this mood.*

The outbreak of the Civil War affected everyone and every institution in the south. Kentucky Masonic College was no different. Enrollment quickly receded and mounting deficits became problematic. Morris had taken over the leadership for the College. He also continued his efforts to strengthen the Conservator's movement, but both began to weaken as the Civil War began to take its toll.

Although greatly admired by many, there were also substantial naysayers that tried to undermine Morris' initiatives in masonry. There were those still doubtful about the nature of a Masonic organization, like the Order of the Eastern Star that allowed women as members. Other critics included lodges from states, such as Michigan and even Kentucky, that did not want a standardized system of rules and regulations as suggested by the Conservator's movement. Lastly, people such as editor, Charles W. Moore of the *Boston Freemasons' Magazine*, questioned the legitimacy of the conferred LL.D. degree to Dr. Morris and called it a "gimmick."

Morris was disappointed with these criticisms but not deterred. He had diligently and faithfully dedicated himself to the cause of freemasonry. In doing so, he had spent his lifetime making contacts and friends from Presidents of the United States to politicians, farmers, preachers, and masons across the country. People loved and admired Dr. Rob Morris and were grateful for the community service and devotion to an organization that reached out from the smallest of pioneer communities to the largest of metropolitan areas.

The home at LaGrange provided the first sense of real stability for the Morris family. The town was large enough to be entertaining and educational for the children and supportive enough for Charlotte to maintain her household duties. But, there was a hazardous incident that almost caused Rob to gather up the family and move.

According to Morris' great grandson, Dr. Robert Fitch, Morris had traveled to Springfield, Illinois for a Grand Lodge meeting and met Abraham

Rob Morris's desk is part of the Morris collection of furniture in his home that is preserved as a historic site in LaGrange by the Order of the Eastern Star.

Morris's dog, Leo, was always by his side and accompanied him on walks through LaGrange.

Morris's interest in numismatics resulted in his own newspaper
publication on the subject when he lived in LaGrange.

Part of Morris's rare coin collection.

Lincoln, just prior to the presidential elections in 1860. Lincoln complimented the Masonic group that Morris was with regarding their position on the Southern political trends (Rule, 1922, p. 93.) A year later, on September 18, 1861, Kentucky's neutrality was compromised by Southern troops from Tennessee. Soon thereafter, November 7, 1861, while Morris visited Crown Point, Indiana on a Masonic lecture, his home in LaGrange was torched by Confederate guerillas. Fortunately, there was a detachment of Union soldiers nearby who were able to salvage some of his Masonic literature.

Morris withdrew his membership from Fortitude Lodge in LaGrange and prepared to move his family to New York, but something changed his mind. In July 1862, he was called into military service by Governor Magoffin as Provost Marshall of Oldham County and surrounding areas. Although a pacifist at heart, Morris took on the responsibility. The next month, he was commissioned a Colonel in the Union Army with orders to organize a regiment of Home Guards in order to defend New Castle.

There was a detachment of Confederate soldiers being recruited in Henry County by Captain George M. Jessee, Co.A of the Kentucky Confederate volunteers. Morris was called up to New Castle to stop the recruitment efforts. There was a tense moment where engagement almost took place between Morris' Home Guard and Jessee' recruits. However, it was said that Morris placed himself between the cannoneers and Southerners, and shouted "Don't fire men! These are our brothers!" and the two sides negotiated a stand-down (op. cit., p. 95-98.)

As the war subsided, the Conservator Movement was met with the skepticism from a country where Civil War had created distrust, hate, and resentment. The movement was seen as a "secret association of Master Masons within the body of Master Masons, designed to control in a vital point the action of the entire body of craftsmen" (op. cit.,p. 146.) Although discouraged, Morris did not apologize for the Conservator Movement, but saw it as an initiative that helped to revive Masonic principles.

By the mid-1860s, Morris turned his attention to the fulfillment of his longtime dream to visit the Holy Land. In 1866, Morris gave his blessing and endorsement to his friend, Robert Macoy, to take over the organization of the Eastern Star, so Morris could raise funds for his trip to the Holy Lands. Morris continued his massive correspondences, lectures, and writings. He also loved the science of numismatics and published from LaGrange newspaper on the subject. Symbols, coinage, and geology were an important part of masonic rituals and the prospect of traveling to the birthplace, where these mystic symbols were embedded in ancient history, had enormous appeal. A trip to the Holy Land for Morris meant a "visit Palestine, the mother-land of ancient affiliations" in "Masonic rituals" (Morris, 1876, p. 12.) It would clarify the meaning of symbols and their role in the Masonic rituals while providing authentic experiences to the birthplace of the Masonic fraternity.

Foyer of the Rob Morris home in LaGrange.

CHAPTER TEN
Trip to the Holy Land

Morris' first effort to the Holy Land was thwarted by a fire in 1854. Funded through a loan from the Grand Lodge of Kentucky for $1,000, he met with a disaster in New York City. He described the incident in a letter to Charlotte.

Boston, Massachusetts, November 26, 1854

My Dear Wife

I commence today writing to you and will write every Sunday. I left Hickman Tuesday morning on the Aleck Scott, got to New York Sunday evening at 3 o'clock. I have seen John and am now at Charlotte's. They are all well and in good spirits. Charlotte lives in the finest house I ever was in. Dr. Wilson is doing well and making money. Bro. John is out of business again owing to the hard times which are very distressing. How poor folks live here I don't see. Flour is twelve dollars a barrel, wood five dollars a cord. Corn a dollar a bushel.

You will be sorry to hear that Judson's Hotel was burnt up the morning after I got there and I lost my baggage and all except the clothes I had on and my overcoat. My shirts, flute, books, watch and everything in the trunk burned. Also Bro. Meriwether's watch. Lucky I didn't bring the Accordeons. I sent a newspaper to John that had an account of the fire and write to him to send it to you that you may read it. We ought to be thankful that I escaped with my life.

I directed Mr. Leonard to hand you all the money he may collect. This is for you to buy what you want to pay Freeman and to pay John's loan and tuition bills. Also to pay the store bills at Feliciana if they send them to you. I think there will be more than a hundred dollars to you from Leonard.

I find business matters in New York encouraging but I will write to you more about that next Sunday and will also let you know what time to look for me ... I think you had better hire Mr. Freeman's girl but I leave that with you. I told him that any agreement you made with him would be all right.

Sixteen years later, with the family now settled in LaGrange, it seemed the time for Morris to plan the trip again. To collect funds for the trip, Morris decided to offer curio cabinets for people that would be filled with specimens from the Holy Land that would have Biblical and Masonic illustration. In the following, Morris described his fundraising efforts in detail.

> Those contributors who advance ten dollars, each shall be supplied with one hundred and fifty objects from the Holy Land, including specimens of the ancient building-stone of Jerusalem, Joppa, and Tyre; shells form the sea of Galilee and Joppa; agates from the Arabian deserts; ancient coins; rock-salt from Usdum; an herbarium of ten plants; the traditional corn, wine and oil of Masonry; earth from the clay-grounds near Succoth, etc., etc.

> Contributors of five dollars, three dollars, and two dollars, respectively, are promised smaller cabinets composed of similar objects; those of one dollar, the journal of the Expedition. A map of the Holy Land, arranged for Masonic purposes, was also a portion of the premiums promised.

> Having decided upon the plan of appeal, I visited one hundred and thirty lodges in Indiana, Iowa, Kentucky, Illinois, West Virginia, Nebraska and New York and addressed the fraternity. I began by occupying an hour or two with recitations of Masonic poems, such as the Level and the Square, the Letter G., the Holy Bible, Our Vows, the Drunkard's Grave, the Five Points of Fellowship, the Emblems of the Craft, etc. and then laid before them my propositions for a Masonic mission to the Holy Land (Morris, 1876, p. 14.)

Morris' appeal netted him $9,631 from 3,782 contributors. From this sum, he calculated the expenses as follows:

> Out of this, according to my proposals, provision was made for two years' support of my family; my own expenses, and those of my agent, Mr. G. W. Bartlett, while collecting the money; the expenses of the Oriental tour, for myself and Mr. Thomson; freights upon shipments of specimens; printing six issues of the Holy Land Journal for 3,782 contributors; printing catalogues, etc; and preparing, labeling, packing, and forwarding nearly 70,000 specimens (op. cit.,p. 15.)

Morris's membership paper to the Fortitude Lodge in LaGrange.

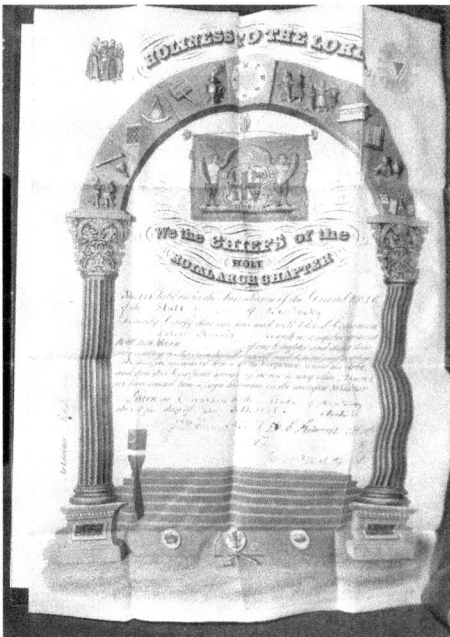

Morris's membership paper for the Royal Arch.

Morris's Knights Templar membership paper. Morris carried all three of his Masonic papers in his billfold as he travelled, both nationally and internationally.

Curio cabinets such as these were used as fundraisers that contained items collected by Morris on his Holy Land trip. *Courtesy of The Grand Chapter of Kentucky, OES.*

Close up of the curio cabinets with items from the Holy Land.
Courtesy of The Grand Chapter of Kentucky, OES.

Shells, wood and a pine cone that Morris collected from his trip to
the Holy Land. *Courtesy of The Grand Chapter of Kentucky, OES.*

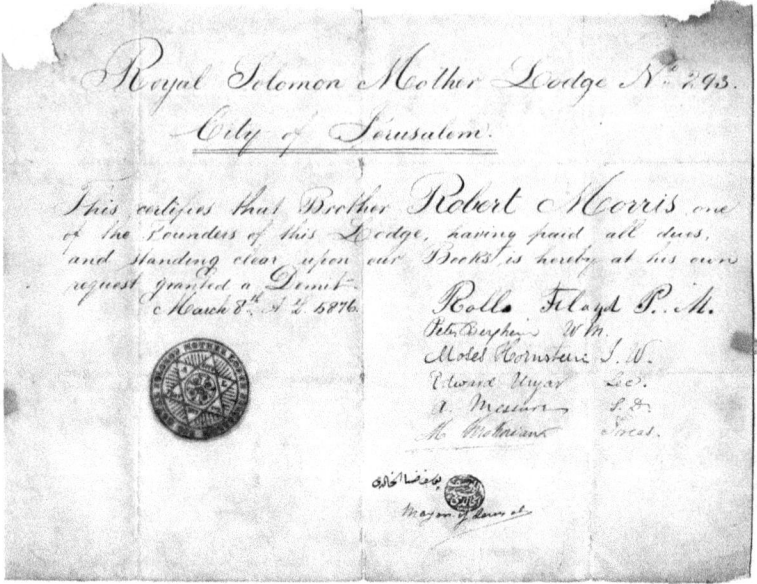

Morris's membership paper to the Royal Solomon Mother Lodge in Jerusalem which later disbanded in the early 20th Century. *Courtesy of the Grand Chapter of Kentucky, OES.*

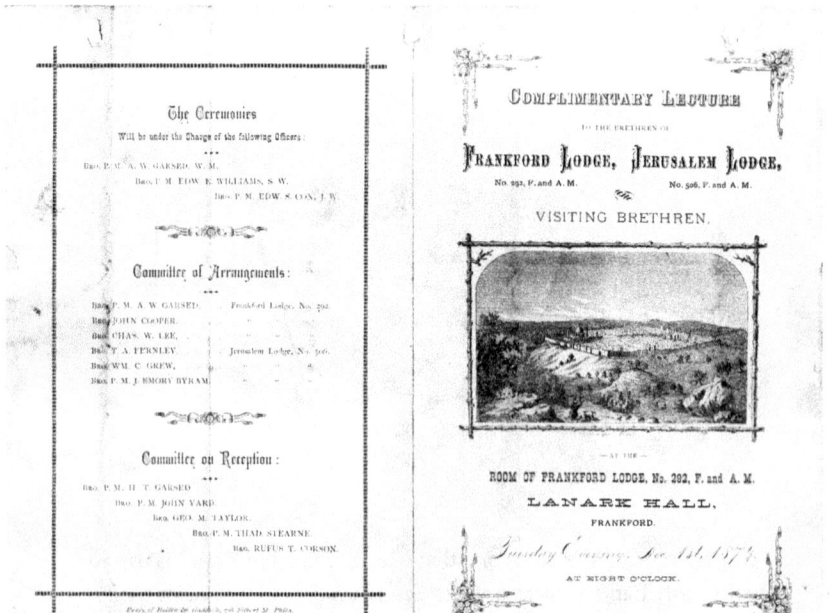

Lecture program by Morris on experiences from the Holy Land.

On Feb. 2, 1868, Morris began his departure from Pier No. 47, North River, NYC on the steamship "France" steered by Captain Grace, a rough-featured, rough-mannered sailor of thirty, taciturn, and gruff, and most ridiculously misnamed (op.cit., p. 25.) For one hundred dollars, he had a first class ticket on the 2,428 ton, 405 foot long vessel, averaging about 1,000 miles a day. There were a total of 84 passengers. Morris, who was always sensitive to sea-sickness, took on his regular practice of vomiting for a few days but then adjusted.

On this journey, Morris made stops to visit various European lodges including the Grand Lodge of England. He crossed France by rail, caught the French steamer "L'Amerique" at Marseilles breezing through the Mediterranean and passing coastline of Italy and Greece. In a scheduled stop in Smyrna, Morris was greeted by fellow Masons where there consisted of seven Lodges and two Royal Arch Chapters. On March 1, 1868, Morris reached Syrian shores and began his investigations of the historic ties of Freemason and the Holy Lands.

In *Freemasonry in the Holy Land or Handmarks of Hiram's Builders* (1876), Morris gave detailed descriptions of the land, people, and customs that he encounters. He was guided by a sheikh and usually traveled by horse. His descriptions of places visited where detailed, colorful, and often humorous. The journal entries were published in his book, but they were also sent home during his adventure and published in newsprint. The following are some of those excerpts:

> And now the noble expanse of water, the Dead Sea, fifty by nine miles in extent, which I am today to visit, breaks before my eyes, fifteen miles distant. It looks from here like a silver sea. Pushing on, past the beggar as naked as the law allows; past the long files of native women, tattooed hideously with blue upon the lower lip and chin, with their breasts indecently exposed, and each having pendent upon the neck one or more heavy silver coins. I now round the last point, and see the village before me, Bethany, memorable as the locality where Lazarus was raised to a second mortality by an enlivening voice and where, on the Wednesday of the Passion Week, two days before his crucifixion, Jesus received the costly offering which a generous woman made him in anointing his body for burial ... (p. 334.)

The seventh and last of the grand Masonic localities that these articles are designed to identify and describe is the City of Jerusalem, upon which sacred place my longing eyes were first directed ... My assistant had been detailed to this point of labor several weeks earlier, and had busied himself in collecting a large quantity of relics and specimens, designed for the cabinets of the zealous craft at home. (p. 365.)

There is an elegant myth connected with the literature of Masonry, to the effect that, upon the arrival of Hiram Abif at Jerusalem, King Solomon conducted him to a point near the junction of the mountains now termed Olivet and Offence, and showed him the range entitled Moriah, which he had selected as the site of his projected temple. On one occasion I sought that spot and endeavored to paint the scene in its natural colors. Moriah was a long, narrow ridge, deeply furrowed by ravines, divided primarily into three peaks by cross valleys, the top of the range rising nearly 400 feet above the bed of the valley of Jehoshaphat on the east, and that of Tyropoeon on the west. Upon that most ill-fitted hill, the king had ordained the construction of his temple; the top to be cut off, the sides to be raised by immense walls, nearly 200 feet high, and the interstices filled in with stone. (p. 373.)

Long before reaching this city, I had resolved, at all hazards, to place the Masonic mark of the Square and Compass conspicuously upon some one of the huge ashlars that make up the wall of the old Templar area on its eastern side (author's note: St. Stephen's Gate). The task was by no means a pleasant one, nor altogether safe ... placing an assistant in the road below, with instructions to keep a vigilant lookout, I marked out my figure and began ... I made my mark deep and bold, as future travelers will not fail to see. It is cut in the fifth stone of the second tier of blocks, counting from the southeast corner of the old Temple-wall to the north. The block is a large one, though not the largest in that part of the structure. (p. 374.)

Excerpt from "My First Day in Joppa"

As I said, breakfast at High XII is an attempt upon the life of a human being, and I attribute my escape from starvation only to the sustenance afforded by Jaffa oranges. When at last breakfast has come,-but let me describe it. First, two of the fish from this harbor, sweet and delicious specimens of the finny tribe whose forefathers did so much to strengthen our Masonic forefathers, as they came floating down this way from the masonic Bay, a hundred miles above here, "one a raft." I ate them both. Next a stewed chicken, stewed to rags as is the custom of this country, but by judicious use of sweet olive oil, in place of butter, well flavored and toothsome; I ate is all. Then comes a plate of cold mutton cut into slices. My eyes being indifferent, I mount my glasses now to "give it a name" and early recognizing it, I ate it all. Next some fried mutton, rather stringy and hard; I ate it all. Now comes a plate of oranges and a cup of coffee, a woman thimble is gigantic in size compared with it. This is my breakfast. Picking my teeth I look out at that fine palm tree younder, my favorite tree of all the trees in the wood. They tell me that the palm bears its fruit (the dates) abundantly in the southern section of Palestine, which is more than it does about Beyrout. There is a large number of palm trees in this vicinity, while the pomegranate, so famous in Masonic symbology, is even more so. I shall secure ample specimens of the wood of both trees.

Having spent the afternoon in a manner suitable to my mission, I sallied forth at the proper hour to fill my appointment with his Excellency, Bro. Nouraddeen Effendi, between whom and myself Freemasonry has established an equality which no other society is capable of. Bro. Adams joined us in the party, and there were present Monsieur Serafia, already named, together with the half dozen clerks and secretaries of the Governor. I showed His Excellency my diploma of the 32d grade, Scottish Rite. I had also my diploma, from my lodge, Fortitude 47, LaGrange, Ky., expressly for this journey; and my firman from the

Sultan. Upon his own part the Kaimakan showed me written evidence of his membership in various loges, and we passed esoterical evidence satisfactory to both. Two hours past by before dinner was commenced, which time was spent in conversation of a varied and pleasing character. His Excellency is one of the best of companions, brother Adams has the art agreeable in perfection, Monsieur Serafia is one of a thousand in making his friends happy, while I found myself both in the mood conversational and musical. Cigarettes and narghilehs were offered in frequency and abundance. The latter is the celebrated water pipe, through which, when the fumes of this mild Turkish tobacco have passed, you can't tell that you are smoking anything. It is this which, according to tradition, King Solomon used while inducting the Queen of Sheba in the art of smoking tobacco. The only drawback connected with its use is the vast expenditure of muscular energy requisite in drawing smoke through it. The first time my associate, Bro. Thomson, used one, he became black in the face from the tremendous effort needful to the occasion, and presented an alarming appearance. I dislike the roar of water which it makes, for I always imagine it is raining torrents outside when I hear one. But I digress.

Dinner was brought in, and in deference to my barbarous American tastes, a table was set with table cloth, plates, etc., instead of putting the dishes on the floor, one by one, and welcoming all to "pitch in." I forgot to say too that nearly all the company had been sitting, during the visit, upon chairs, thought the Kaimakan preferred his couch upon which he sat cross-legged, the natural posture I think of all Orientals, borrowed originally from the camel. But every one, save brother Adams and myself, invariably slipped off their shoes at the door and came into the room in his stocking feet. This is universal even those persons (and there are but few, save the military) who wear boots or gaiters, have a pair of overshoes which they slip off under the circumstances names. The reader will early see then that at a large religious meeting, or at a great man's door-way, the pile of shoes is oftentimes immense. Miserable slipshod affairs, however, they are as a general thing.

Shall I describe the dinner? First came the soup, well made, thickened with rice and containing forced meat balls. Next was a lamb stuffed with rice and roasted whole! This was elegantly cooked, and although I had often read of the dish, it was the first that I had ever seen. It is called in Turkish *pilau*, and with the great is a favorite dish. When I say that it was as good as the first barbecue I ever tasted, under Kentucky beech trees, and that I devoured so much as to make my dreams for several nights of the severest muttony nature, I hope my readers will understand me. Those who do not, can get corroborative evidence from Bro. G. J. Adams, whose exploits in the field of *pilau* excelled my own.

The third course consisted of something fried, no doubt very proper and good, but for some reason my appetite had become very languid and capricious, and I ate but little thereof. Next was a dish of custard in Syrian style, out of which, after the guests had been served, *every one at the table with his own spoon,* pitched in. It was amusing to see with what avidity the Governor and his staff "went in" for that custom in their childhood ways. I fear that it was the only dish they really enjoyed; the restraint of eating off plates in the American style had a depressing effect upon Orientals. With the pudding came confectionary, such as cakes, jellies and the like, in the manufacture of which the Syrians greatly excel. This was followed by coffee, strong and black, without milk or sugar. I forgot to say that an abundance of champagne was served throughout the repast, and that all present, Moslems, Armenians, and Protestants, drank it without religious scruple. It was quite ten o'clock before dinner ended and we retired to our respective abodes.

The trip lasted seven months and Morris returned home to his family in LaGrange on July 21. Although he met many Masons in the Middle East, there was no Grand Lodge established there, so he began a process to do so.

Morris had a strong friendship with William Mercer Wilson, Grand Master of the United Grand Lodge of Canada. He had visited Canada several times and was even involved in settling a dispute issue. The respect was so high for Morris that he had been named as Past Deputy Grand Master.

The relationship between Wilson and Morris enabled Morris to petition the Grand Lodge of Canada for a charter for a Lodge in Jerusalem. By command of the M.W. Bro. W.M. Mercer, Royal Solomon Mother Lodge in the city of Jerusalem was constituted by charter issued by the Grand Lodge of Canada on February 17, 1873. Rob Morris was named the first Master of this Lodge and instructed to observe all the rights and regulations of the Craft.

The purpose of the warrant was to pay homage to the birthplace of freemasonry and revive the Masonic light in its native home. The Grand Master of Canada sent jewels and collars for the officers of the new Lodge. Rob Morris proposed that every Master Mason who was a member of the American-Holy Land Exploration Society (which he had formed from the contributions of supporters for his Holy Land trip) would automatically be an honorary life member without further dues or fees. So was established the first and last Canadian Lodge instituted off Canadian soil. The warrant was sent to Jerusalem and minute book indicated the following members present: by Bro. J. Sheville, S.W., Bro. R. Floyd , J.W., Bro. C.F.T. Drake, Acting Secretary, and Bros. G.M. Powell, S. Bergheim, J. Hilpem, P. Bergheim. The first Meeting was held on May 7, 1873, at King Solomon Quarries underneath the Old City of Jerusalem as The Royal Solomon Mother Lodge No. 293.

Unfortunately, the Lodge did not last. The members did not understand how to operate their Lodge and they were hoping for help and aid from their fellow masons in Canada or North America to come and assist them. An appeal was made from the Jerusalem Lodge to Rob Morris, but the financial burden and time involved was not a possibility for Morris to make the trip. Morris urged the new Lodge to look inward to their own members for instructions. The Jerusalem Lodge fell in disarray over the years and the Canadian Grand Lodge acknowledged the difficulties it had to maintain a Lodge so far away. The warrant for the Lodge was cancelled in March 1907 (Lazar, 2014.)

As Morris completed his lifelong dream by visiting the Holy Land, there was another event that marked Morris' endeavors for perpetuity in the Masonic world. He was crowned the Poet Laureate of Freemasonry for the 19th Century.

CHAPTER 11

The 19ᵗʰ Century Poet Laureate of Freemasonry

On Dec. 17, 1884 Rob Morris was crowned the Poet Laureate of Free-masonry at the Grand Lodge Room of the Masonic Temple in New York. Morris succeeded the 18ᵗʰ Century Poet Laureate, Robert Burns who took the honor in 1787 as the first poet laureate of Freemasonry in Canon-gate Kilwilling Lodge, No. 2, Edinburgh, Scotland.

To achieve the honor of Poet Laureate, a query was sent, over the signatures of the Grand Master, Deputy Grand Master, and Grand Secretary of New York, to over 1,000 Masons in the United States, Canada, and Great Britain to support Morris as Poet Laureate of Freemasonry. The response was overwhelming and immediate: "Crown him, he has earned it; he honors Freemasonry by his pure life, genius, and learning; he has sought through many tribulations the truth!" "Crown him, his single poem, The Level and The Square, demands the laurel wreath!" "Crown Him: let there be no waiting till after death to mark his praise, but honor his grey hairs while he is yet in the land of the living" (Oldham County Historical Society, n.d.)

The ceremony began with a very large procession of the Grand Master of New York, William Brodie, with his Grand Lodge officers who were then accompanied by "guests" from all jurisdictions. The Overture to William Tell was played on the pipe organ. Invocation read by Rev. Howard, a Past Grand Chaplain of Kentucky. Rev. J. Worrall, Past Grand Commander of Kentucky gave a talk on the history of Freemasonry. John R. Collins recited "The Level and the Square." Frank Lawrence, Deputy Grand Master of New York, gave an address about "The Poetry of Freemasonry." The tribute and biography of Morris was read by John Simons, Grand Master of New York which was followed by the Laureation ceremony presented by William A. Brodie. Morris" longtime friend, Robert Macoy chaired the Committee of Arrangements for the crowning of a laurel wreath that was placed upon Morris' head (Ibid.)

By this time, Morris had traveled in three continents, visited more than three thousand lodges, and penned over seventy volumes of work that included close to four hundred poems. He had visited Presidents and Heads of State and established the first Masonic Lodge in Jerusalem. The Order of the Eastern Star that he organized was now flourishing and expanding, offering women a national organization that gave women a local place where they could meet, socialize, network, and provide charitable works to their community.

The largest volume of poems by Morris, *The Poetry of Freemasonry*, contained over four hundred of his compositions, and was published in 1884, the same year that Morris was crowned Poet Laureate. Morris described the collection as being composed "'upon the wing' on horseback, on foot, in coach and in car, at wayside inns and on the sea" (Morris, 1895, p. xiv

Much of Morris' poetry can be described as Carpe diem-pieces written to celebrate an occasion or event. When important events took place in the world of freemasonry, Rob Morris was included as the official to produce a piece of prose or writing. These literary pieces not only solidified a momentous event in history but became tangible evidence of record that could be printed, shared, and saved. An example of these momentous occasions was the union of The Ancient Grand Lodge of Canada with the Grand Lodge of Canada. The Ancient Lodge of Canada was ordained under the Grand Lodge of England and as such operated under the Mother country's Masonic constitution. The Grand Lodge of Canada was created as independent from the English order feeling that Canada should not be subject to English mandates and could operate on its own. The debate over unifying these two lodges lasted many years and finally culminated into a merger as described by Rob Morris in a letter to the editor of "The Masonic Journal" (July, 1858):

> I arrived at Toronto on Tuesday the 13th (July). Brother P.C. Tucker (of Vermont) arrived the same evening. We met the committee on both sides and gave our opinions. Each Grand Lodge adopted the report by an almost unanimous vote, and at 10 o'clock on the 14th Sir Allan MacNab, led his forces into the hall of the Wilson Grand Lodge, and the union was consummated amidst great cheering and mutual congratulations. The basis is—'The Ancient' Grand Lodge is dissolved—its lodges and officers come into The Grand Lodge of Canada with equal honors and privileges, the same as officers and lodges formerly adhering.

To mark the historic event, Morris created the following poem with this introduction: "In the settlement of the long-pending difficulties among the Canadian Masons, the writer was called in, July, 1858, with Philip C. Tucker, Grand Master of Vermont, to suggest proper terms of reconciliation.

The pleasing task being performed, and the union complete, the following lines were read at a banquet that most agreeably terminated the meeting" (Morris, 1875, p. 59).

The Spirit of Union

There never was occasion, and there never was an hour,
When spirits of peace on angel wings so near our heads did soar;
There's no event so glorious on the page of time to appear,
As the union of the Brotherhood, sealed by our coming here.

'Twas in the hearts of many, 'twas in the prayers of some,
That the good old days of Brotherly Love might yet in mercy come;
'Twas whispered in our Lodges, in the E. and S. and W.,
That the time was nigh when the plaintive cry our God would hear
and bless.

But none believed the moment of fruition was at hand;
How could we deem so rich a cup was waiting our command?
It came like rain in summer drought, on drooping foliage poured,
And bade us look henceforth for help, in all our cares, to God!

The news has gone already upon every wind of Heaven;
The wire, the press, the busy tongue, the intelligence has given;
And everyone who heard it and who loves the Sons of Peace,
Has cried, "Praise God, the God of Love! May God this union bless!"

Vermont takes up the story—her "old man eloquent,"—
Long be his days among us, on deeds of mercy spent,—
He speaks for the Green Mountains, and you heard him say last night,
"Bless God that I have lived till now to see this happy sight!"

Kentucky sends you greeting,—from her broad and generous bound,
Once styled of all the western wild, "the Dark and Bloody Ground;"
She cries aloud, "God bless you! Heaven's dews be on your shed,
Who first took care to be in the right, then boldly went ahead!"

From yonder constellation, from the Atlantic to the West,
Where the great pines of Oregon rear up their lofty crest,

From the glory glades of Florida, from Minnesota's plain,
Each voice will say, "Huzza! Huzza! This Craft is one again!"

Old England soon will hear it; not always will the cry
Of suffering Brothers meet her ear, and she pass coldly by;
There's a chord in British hearts vibrates to every tale of wrong,
And she will send a welcome and a Brother's hand ere long.

Then joyful be this meeting, and many more like this,
As year by year shall circle round, and bring you added bliss;
In quarry, hill and temple, peace, nor cruel word or thought
Disturb the perfect harmony the gracious God has wrought.

But while your walls are thus compact, your cement strong and good,
Your workmen diligent and just, a mighty Brotherhood,
Remember, Brethren, o'er the earth, and on the raging sea,
How many a heart there is to-night that sighs, "Remember me!"

By the sign the world knows nothing of, but to our eyes so clear,-
By the token known in darkest hour, that tells a Brother dear,-
By the sacred vow and word, and by "the hieroglyphic bright,"
Remember all, the wide world round, who claim your love to-night.

The following poem was written to hail the event when Dr. Kane, an Artic navigator, left New York to search for Sir John Franklin who had been missing from an exploration undertaken to the North Pole. Dr. Kane set out in his boat with the Masonic Square and Compass printed on the foresails. Unfortunately, Sir John was never found (Morris, 1895, p. 169.)

The Pursuit of Franklin

Midst polar snows and solitude,
Eight weary years the voyager lies,
Ice-bound upon the frozen flood,
While expectation vanishes;
Ah! Many a hopeless tear is shed
For Franklin, numbered with the dead!

Midst joys of home, and well earned fame,
Young, healthful, honored, there is one

Who pines to win a nobler name,
And feels his glory but begun;
His heart is with the voyager, lost
Midst polar solitude and frost.

The voice from off the frozen flood
Appeals in trumpet tone for aid:
'Tis heard, 'tis answered,—swift abroad
The flag is hung, the sail is spread;
That sail on whose pure face we see
Thy symbol, honored Masonry!

Away, on glorious errand, now,
Thous hero of a sense of right!
Success be on they gallant brow,
Thou greater than the sons of might!
Thy flag, the banner of the free,
Oh, may it lead to victory!

Is there some chain of sympathy
Flung thus across the frozen seas?
Is there some strange, mysterious tie,
That joins these daring men?—there is!
This, honored, healthful, free from want,
Is bound to that in Covenant!

The Lodge Welcome to Ladies was written as a welcome to women in the new Adoptive Masonry, Order of the Eastern Star, (Morris, 1895, p. 336.)

Lodge Welcome to Ladies (first two and last verse)

It is in our hearts dear Sisters
While the Mason chain is bright,
To give our warmest welcome
To the best-beloved tonight.
To the Wife, so fondly cherished,
To the daughter, sister, true,
To the faithful, tender-hearted
Shall I say the word? to you.

Then hail! Adoptive Masonry,
That brings us here together;
May manly arms 'round lovely forms
Protect from stormy weather;
And when, adown the hill of life,
Our tottering feet shall go,
May our weary steps be comforted,—
Shall I say the word?—by you.

Morris attended many cornerstone dedications and produced poems such
as this one, for the Chamber of Commerce building at Peoria, Illinois on
June 3, 1875.

To-day as Then

How ever fresh and vigorous
The tie that binds these men!
Three thousand years,—and yet as strong
And true to-day as then!
The tears, the sighs of broken hearts,
The wails of dying men,
Appeal to sympathy as true
And strong to-day as then!

The arm Divine maintains its power.
The All-seeing Eye its ken,
As gracious and as wonderful
And wise to-day as then.

Lay deep the stone; apply the Square,
The Level and the Plumb;
Happy the work and bright the day
When mystic craftsmen come.

According to Morris, 'Leaning Toward Each Other' was first read at a
banquet following the inauguration of the Crawford Equestrian Statue
of George Washington at Richmond, Va. Not long afterward Morris, visiting President Buchanan at the White House by invitation, was requested to read the same poem before an audience that included the President,

Vice-President (John C. Breckenridge), the Secretary of State Lewis Cass, and the Honorable B. B. French. All of the men were Freemasons.

Leaning Toward Each Other (first three verses)

The jolts of life are many,
As we dash along the track;
The ways are rough and rugged,
And our bones they sorely rack.
We're tossed about,
We're in and out,
We make a mighty pother-
Far less would be
Our pains, if we
Would lean toward each other!

Behold that loving couple,
Just mated for their life-
What care they for the joltings,
That happy man and wife!
The cars may jump,
Their heads may bump
And jostle one another;
They only smile,
And try the while
To lean toward each other!

Woe to the luckless pilgrim
Who journeys all alone!
Well said the wise King Solomon-
"Two better is than one!!"
For when the ground's
Most rugged found,
And great's the pain and pother,
He cannot break
The sorest shake
By leaning on each other!

Morris gave eulogies and composed poems for funerals. He traveled across the United States, often doing so. When he could not make a funeral, he sent a poem in the deceased's honor. The saddest occasion for a poem was the one he wrote for his daughter, Ella Wilson Morris, who died after a long illness, at age 20 on July 29, 1877. Her marker lies on the East side of her father's grave at the Valley of Rest cemetery in LaGrange. This composition was written a year before she passed on June 15, 1876.

The Father to the Dying Daughter

Dear Ella, as you watch the flowers of June,
And wear away the summer days in pain,
Do you not often think of seasons gone,
And wish that childhood's days were back again?

I know you do,- they were such sunny days.
Your happy girlhood never knew a care;
Sisters and brothers shared you merry plays,
Your parents took of all your pains the share.

How sweet the moments fled! We used to sing
Such joyful melodies! When evening fell
To father's knee you little hand would cling,
And prayers went up to Him we loved so well.

We sang sweet "Mary at the Saviour's tomb,"
We sang "thus far the Lord hath led us on,"
And in dear mother's own domestic room
We kissed good night, and then to bed were gone.

Ah, Ella, there is nothing left like this!
In womanhood there dwell such woe and pain;
Had we but known it was our time of bliss,—
Oh that my children were but young again!

Gray-haired and sad, I meditate today,
My tears fast dropping through the lonely hour;
Is there not somewhere, somewhere, far away,
A home where bitter memoires come no more?
We do believe there is, we will believe—
You learned such faith, my daughter, at my knee;

The Holy One, who never can deceive,
Assures us of a blest eternity.

Read it again—"All tears are wiped away,"
The saints with crowns and harps all radiant stand,
The Lam sits on the throne, and endless day
And jubilant song pervade the happy Land.

Then bow with patience, Dearest, 'neath your load;
A mighty Saviour waits to be your Guide;
Jesus the painful pilgrimage hath trod,
Eternal life and light with Him that died.

The greatest number of poems Morris composed underscored meaning of the symbolic images fundamental to the definition of freemasonry. These poems took a particular symbol and helped commit to memory the meaning of the images in a lyrical way. His classic "The Level and the Square" written in 1854, early in his career, was the most well-known and recited poem that he composed. Morris stated that there had been fifteen musical compositions that had been set to the poem.

The Level and the Square

We meet upon the Level and we part upon the Square;
What words of precious meaning those words Masonic are!
Come, let us contemplate them! They are worthy of a thought;
In the very walls of Masonry the sentiment is wrought.

We meet upon the Level, thought from every station come,
The rich man from his palace and the poor man from his home;
For the rich must leave his wealth and state outside the Mason's door,
And the poor man finds his best respect upon the Checkered Floor.
We act upon the Plumb—'tis the orders of our Guide,
We walk upright in virtue's way and lean to neither side;
Th' All-Seeing Eye that reads our hearts doth bear us witness true;
That we still try to honor God and give each man his due.

We part upon the Square, for the world must have its due;
We mingle with the multitude, a faithful Band and true;

But the influence of our gatherings in memory is green,
And we long upon the Level to renew the happy scene.

There's a World where all are equal—we are hurrying towards it fast,
We shall meet upon the Level there, when the gates of Death are
passed.
We shall stand before the Orient, and our Master will be there,
To try the blocks we offer with His own unerring Square.

We shall meet upon the Level, there, but never thence depart;
There's a Mansion—'tis all ready for each trusting, faithful heart;
There's a Mansion and a Welcome, and a multitude is there
Who have met upon the Level, and been tried upon the Square

Let us meet upon the Level, then while laboring patient here;
Let us meet and let us labor, thought the labor be severe;
Already in the Western sky the signs bid us prepare
To gather up on Working Tools and part upon the Square.

Hands round, ye faithful Brotherhood, the bright fraternal chain,
We part upon the Square below, to meet in Heaven again!
What words of precious meaning those words Masonic are,—
We meet upon the Level and we part upon the Square.

Between 1859 and 1860, Morris created The National Schools of Instruction on Freemasonry and held at least five sessions on these schools across the country. According to Morris, the schools were well attended and contained lessons on conducting lodges, rituals, etc. The following is a valedictory poem (first and last verses) composed by Morris on the last day of the school session held in Louisville (Morris, 1875, p. 52.)

The Teacher to His Pupils

From the hills of old Virginia, from the meadows fat and rare,
From the banks of broad Ohio, and of others broad and fair,
From the borders of our neighboring states, true neighbors each they
stand,
You have come responsive, Brothers, and have gripped me by the
hand.

Then each Farewell! Bear homeward Light our fathers well approved.
Set up the Pillars, rear the Walls; 'twas work our fathers loved;
Time will your fond devotions to unending ages tell;
God will o'ersee and bless you! Brothers, faith fully, farewell!

That last poem in this chapter is an imagery poem. Morris wrote a whole series of poems on the meaning of symbols that were used in Masonic ritual. The cedar tree is symbol for everlasting life in Freemasonry. Morris enclosed a leaflet from a cedar tree in his correspondence and a cedar branch was enclosed with the deceased in the casket (Morris, 1895, p. 269.)

The Cedar Tree (first two verses)

Droops thy bough, oh Cedar-tree,
Like you dear, you aged form,
Droops thy bough in sympathy
For the wreck of life's sad storm!
Sad, indeed, his weary age,—
Lonely, now his princely home,
And the thoughts his soul engage,
Are of winter and the tomb!

Twas for this, oh Cedar-tree,
Verdant midst the wintry strife,
'Twas for this he planted thee,
Type of an immortal life,—
That when round his grave in tears,
Brothers in their art combine,
From the store they foliage bears,
Each may cast a portion in!

Poet Laureate of Freemasonry program for Rob Morris, 1884, outside cover.

Poet Laureate of Freemasonry program for Rob Morris, 1884, inside cover.

their voices through all time to thy enduring praise.

Z. C. LUSE, Past Grand Master,
IOWA CITY, IOWA.

I most heartily and cheerfully concur with yourself and the other distinguished fraters in the matter of crowning our good and faithful brother, ROB MORRIS, as Poet Laureate of Freemasonry. His poem, "The Level and The Square," if he had never written another line, would entitle him to that distinguished honor, so long delayed but now about to be conferred upon him.

D. MURRAY LYON, Grand Secretary,
(author of various Masonic works of standard character),
EDINBURGH, SCOTLAND.

I desire heartily to reciprocate the feelings by which the projectors of the honorarium are animated in paying respect to my very old, warm-hearted, and heartily esteemed brother, ROB MORRIS, LL.D. He has indeed, for many years, been the Poet Laureate of Freemasonry, and well deserves the laurel crown. Early in my Masonic career I was brought in contact with Dr. MORRIS, and it was he who gave the incentive to that taste for Masonic literature which led to the production of my widely known "History of Freemasonry in Scotland," published some ten years ago.

I should much like to be with you at the coronation, but my duties here prevent it, and I must rest contented with this opportunity of saying how highly I appreciate ROB MORRIS' sterling worth and ability as a man, as a Mason, and as a poet.

CLIFFORD P. MAC CALLA, Junior Grand Warden,
PHILADELPHIA, PA.

I sincerely regret that my engagements are such as to preclude the possibility of a personal participation in the pleasures of "Coronation Day," December 17, 1884, when Past Grand Master Brother ROB MORRIS, LL.D., will receive from his brethren the laurel crown he has so richly merited, and be hailed the Poet Laureate of Freemasonry. It was an honor for him to have been Grand Master of Masons of Kentucky, but it was a greater honor to have been the author of "The Level and the Square."

EDWIN G. MARTIN, Grand Commander,
ALLENTOWN, PA.

I am rejoiced to have this opportunity of contributing a leaf to the laurel crown you are weaving for Brother MORRIS.

The true poet is indeed a workman who needs not blush for his work. The hero accomplishes his part once for all, but the poet makes his valor immortal and sublime unto all generations. Affection, in the lonely recesses of its sphere, breathes out its solicitude, and offers its life in self-sacrifice: the poet assumes divine powers, and sets the deed upon a pedestal where all may see, admire and copy. To write the songs of a people is to become the teacher

laureate crown speaks not, like the iron crown of the warrior, of death, or even as the coronet of gold and gems, of merely material things, but of life, of hope, of joy, of immortality. That its wearer may attain to all these, in the highest sense, is my sincere wish.

ABE MARX, Grand Treasurer,
TUCSON, ARIZONA.

My best wishes will be with you in the proposed coronation, and I trust the occasion will be a happy one.

DAVID P. MASON, Grand Master,
ALBANY, OREGON.

All my Masonic life I have been a devoted admirer of Brother MORRIS' writings. Whenever I read them, I seem to apprehend the true spirit of Masonry breathed out in every line.

J. J. MASON, Grand Secretary,
HAMILTON, ONT.

I regret exceedingly that I find it will be impossible for me to be present at the ceremony in honor of the Masonic Poet Laureate, M.W. Brother ROB MORRIS, on the evening of the 17th inst. From the formation of our Grand Lodge down to the present time Brother MORRIS has been our steadfast, faithful friend, and in his wanderings up and down our jurisdiction he has made many warm personal friends among those who heretofore knew him only by reputation, and I am one of the band.

I am glad that the movement to do him honor promises to be so successful, and I again express my regret that I cannot assist personally in the ceremony.

ZELOTES H. MASON, Past Grand Master,
APOPKA, FLA.

May the G. A. O. T. U. preserve the life of our venerable brother to enjoy the honorarium you are preparing for him, and which he has so honestly merited.

C. T. McCLENACHAN, G.·.C.·. in C.·.
(author of Revised Edition of Mackey's Encyclopedia and other meritorious productions),
NEW YORK.

Your proposal cannot meet with a too warm response from me. I bow to genius. I bow to the Masonic educator. Who in this latter respect has done more than Brother MORRIS? He has riveted the attention of the entire Brotherhood upon the ennobling instructions of Masonry, through the beautiful and touching sentiments that pervade his songs and poetry.

I only regret that this could not be made a *national*, nay, a *world-wide* matter, for the affair is one that cannot fail of the indorsement of the Craft universal.

CHARLES T. McCOY, Grand Secretary,
ABERDEEN, DAK.

I am in receipt of your circular letter, extending an invitation to be present at the ceremonies attending

Examples of letters written by Masons from all over the world to support the nomination of Morris as Poet Laureate of Freemasonry in the 19th Century.

FUNERAL NOTICE.

ELLA, *beloved daughter of Dr. and Mrs. Robert Morris, died in much peace at 9 A. M., Sunday, July 29, 1877, aged 20 years.*

The friends of the family and citizens generally are respectfully notified that the interment will be made at the LaGrange Cemetery Monday morning. Religious exercises will be held at the Baptist Church, of which she was a devoted member, commencing at half past 10 A. M. The teachers and scholars of the various Sunday Schools of LaGrange are particularly invited to join in a mark of respect to this dear young lady who, during all her residence here of 17 years, never failed in attendance upon Sunday School.

" Thanks be to God, which giveth us the victory through our Lord Jesus Christ "

Rob and Charlotte's daughter Ella Morris's obituary. Ella is buried next to her parent's gravestones located in the Valley of Rest Cemetery in LaGrange.

CHAPTER TWELVE
Later Years and Life Eternal

As the Morris' children grew up, the family faced the trials and tribulations of life, with one of the most tragic when their daughter, Ella, passed at age 20. There was also a small incident where Ruth Electa was involved with a man that her father and family highly disapproved. The family intervened and the relationship was broken. Later Ruth began dating John Mount, son of James and Amanda Mount in LaGrange. In the following, Morris wrote a letter to his future son-in-law, John Mount, giving his consent to marry Ruth:

Nov. 29, 1877, Cincinnati, Ohio at the New Gibson House, Fourth and Walnut St.

Mr. John F. Mount:

My Dear Friend,

It affords me pleasure to answer your letter and say that if Ruth has given you her consent, mine shall not be wanting.

My friendship with your father until his death, and with your excellent mother, and my long acquaintance with you gives me the hope that this new tie will bind at all together more closely than ever and make a union that nothing but death can break.

Your friend
Rob Morris

John Mount's parents resided at 106 N. Second Ave., in LaGrange which is now the J.C. Barnett Library & Archives of the Oldham County History Center. James Mount served as a local constable as well as the local city board. Amanda Railey Mount's grandmother was the sister to Thomas Jefferson's mother. John and Amanda were good friends with Henry Clay who visited their home in LaGrange several times. Amanda donated a parcel of land for the construction of a Presbyterian Church which was well attended by the Morris family. Rob Morris referred once to the church saying, "There are two things dear to my heart, my Presbyterian Church and Freemasonry." The church, also located on the Oldham County History Center property, now serves as the Rob Morris Chapel Education Center.

During this period, Morris set lyrics to hymns that were published. Some of these hymns are still sung at OES and Masonic gatherings. The trip to the

Holy Land did not conclude Morris' lust for travel. He kept visiting Lodges and attending OES and masonic meetings in North America, with his wife Charlotte, by his side. They traveled by railroad from Maine to Oregon. He was a much sought-after guest lecturer, delivering poems and speeches in many different venues, from funerals to churches to masonic events. He suffered a minor stroke in 1875 which set him back from his travels for a while but resumed and by 1877 was back on the road again. During these trips, Rob kept in touch with his children, writing letters, some of which were directed to his grandchildren. This one is directed to his grandson, Robbie Mount, son of John and Ruth:

Missoula, Montana, Nov. 1, 1887

Dear Little Boy

Your letter of Oct 25 made me glad. I sent you a railroad map. The places marked with a pen are places I have visited. Tomorrow I go to Spokane Falls which is in Washington Territory. After that I travel to Spokane, Colfax, Farmington, Dayton, Walla Walla and then into Oregon to Pendleton and Baker City. Write to me in the enclosed envelope.

I see the soldiers are hurrying to Billings where bad Indian, Sword Beaver, is making his brags. Two companies of soldiers left here yesterday for Billings. Mr. Sword Beaver had better keep quiet or they will shoot him as quick as they would a wolf.

This is a beautiful place. The high mountains are grand. There are many wild mountain goats around here but I never have seen one.

I hope you read my letter in the Owl. I shall write another one soon. Get the paper and cut them out for your Scrap Book.

Your loving

Grandpa

I am very sorry to hear that Grandma Mount is so sick. Tell her so for me.

Other family letters indicate that Rob and Charlotte resided in various places for several months, usually during the winter.

By the early 1880s, Rob Morris was a household name. As Poet Laureate of Freemasonry and as the recognized founder of the popular Order of the Eastern Star, he was a revered figure. To this effect, OES Chapters began celebrating Morris' birthday. On August 31, 1881, The Daily Monitor newspaper from Ft. Scott, Kansas reported "a large number of prominent ladies and gentlemen from adjoining cities of Parson, Iola, Girard, Paola, and other points" visited Ft. Scott to celebrate the natal day of Rob Morris. The paper goes one to define the importance of OES:

> Out of these and other social evolutions which have been peculiar to the present century; as for instance the increasing social importance of women, the spirit of the age which was demanding an extension of woman's influence and usefulness, spring the Order.
>
> In fact the same social revolution which had called women to the responsible positions of author, preacher, teacher, physician and made her a factor in all of the social and intellectual activities of society, revolted at the notion that Mason's wives and daughters should be a mere affix to the order of Masonry with no standing except that contained in a precarious memory and no privileges, which might not be abridged by a recalcitrant husband or father. To obviate this difficulty and render practical the demand of the times without violating the ancient and well established law of the Order that woman should became a Mason, the chapter devised out of the germ suggested by Rob Morris.

From this point forward, the natal day of Morris is celebrated by most OES Chapters.

The last couple of years found Morris close to his home in LaGrange. His finances somewhat limited, a Masonic "thank you" offering circulated through the Order of the Eastern Star to initiate a fund that could support Morris. A plan was devised for the fund as follows:

> First: Shares in the Fund are $5 each, but several persons may be united in one share at their pleasure.
>
> Second: The money is to be permanently invested in interest paying bonds for the sole benefit of Brother Morris and his wife.
>
> Third: An elegant, engraved Certificate will be returned to each shareholder.

Fourth: An elegant Medal in bronze will be presented each shareholder.

Fifth: Subscriptions will be considered as due and owing not later than November, 1884, but may be redeemed at once, at the choice of the subscriber.

Sixth: The amount subscribed may be sent the Grand Worthy Patron of the Grand Chapter having jurisdiction, or sent direct to Dr. Rob Morris, LaGrange, Kentucky, at the pleasure of the subscriber. Remittances should be made by money orders, postal notes, checks or in registered letters.

Seventh: A full List of Contributors, with the amounts, etc., will be published, and a copy sent to each subscriber.

Description of the Medal: This is of bronze, the size of one half dollar. Upon the obverse is a medallion head of Rob Morris, with name and age. Upon the reverse, with an appropriate emblem, is the inscription, Masonic Gratitude, and the history of the transaction (Oldham County Historical Society, 1888.)

Morris remained in fairly good health until six weeks before his death on July 31, 1888. He was survived by wife Charlotte and his six remaining children: John Anson Morris, Charlotte Fales Morris who had married Honorable H. G. Goodrich, Dr. Alfred W. Morris, Jr., Sarah Morris who had married Latimer Hitt and Ruth Electa Morris who married John Mount.

Funeral ceremonies took place in LaGrange and were conducted by the Grand Lodge of Kentucky, Past Grange Master Hiram Bassett who was a close friend of Morris. A special train carried brethren from Louisville. The Knight Templars were present. At the home, a number of Pilgrim Knights (of the Palm and Shell) organized by Morris performed mystic ceremonies. A Guard of Honor consisted of Past Commanders conveyed the casket to the Presbyterian Church where there was a male choir, led by Brother Smythe and assisted by a number of brethren and accompanied by organ played by Brother Wm. T. Boden.

There were numerous others who spoke and then the Grand Secretary of Kentucky read a poem that Morris had given him and requested it be read at the first Masonic gathering after his death.

A Message from the Grave (Partial verse)

Brothers in June or December
Honoring the memory of dear St. John,
Then let some kind participant remember
The name of him who wrote this, but is gone;
Let some kind brother rise, while all are silent,
And with deep pathos and fond friendship say:
He was a mason, gentle, true, not violent,
And loved old things that do not pass away

In 1889, a year after Morris died there were 2,097 Masonic Lodges in the United States with 147,827 members. During that same year, an appeal by Morris' friend and executor, H. R. Coleman, went out to Brethren to help pay Morris' debts.

My Dear Brethen

Dr. Rob. Morris, whose name will ever be a household word and a credit to American Freemasonry, gave his life, with all his learning, strength and means to the cause of Masonry, and died poor. He left a heavy mortgage on all his books, library, etc., to pay a debt which he contracted for printing, solely for Freemasonry. It has become my sad duty to administer on those things to pay that debt, in justice to his creditors and for the honor of his good name, I have therefore selected a number of Lodges—yours being one of them—feeling confident that if I would appeal to you, you would respond at once (not with a donation, I do not ask that) and provide yourselves with some of those books, which I will furnish you for less than they are worth.

I have about sixteen sets of what is called the Masonic Library, each set containing fifteen octavo volumes, averaging 385 pages to the volume, bound in leather (full sheep), unused, only shelf-worn, forming a Masonic library of the very best selections of standard Masonic literature extant, and, of rare value; the whole containing 5,778 large pages. I will sell to any brother, or to your Lodge, a set of the above for $20.00 until all are gone.

I have on hand, also, about 500 copies of Dr. Morris' Masonic Poems, complete, in heavy manila cover, and printed with the same plates as those for $5.00 a copy (Oldham County Historical Society, 1888.)

In addition to the appeal to help settle Morris' debts, there was a collection made by both Eastern Star Chapters and Masonic Lodges for Morris' grave marker and monument. On May 29, 1891 there was a dedication and unveiling of the monument gravestone for Morris at the Valley of Rest Cemetery

Rob Morris' wife, Charlotte, went through great sacrifices as Morris' zealous efforts kept him away from his family in their early years of marriage. Charlotte persevered and with the help of their eldest son, John, and with Morris' appointment to the Ky. Masonic College, the family embraced life at their permanent home at LaGrange.

There is no doubt that Morris' efforts could not have been as successful without Charlotte and John's help. Morris' commitment to the fraternal order of Freemasonry and his faith cast a wide net that provided a respected organized network where men and women could come together and work on charitable causes locally, nationally, and internationally. By the early 20th Century, the Order of the Eastern Star was known worldwide. Women, such as Red Cross founder, Clara Barton, one of the most widely respected women in the world, had become an OES member with an OES chapter named in her honor from her hometown of Oxford, Massachusetts.

In Reflection

Rob Morris began his writing during the Antebellum period of American history when American literature was being defined. Sculpted by writers, such as Ralph Waldo Emerson, self-reliance, and experience were seen as effective as intellect. With this new literary direction, compositions developed around the context of divisive issues such as westward expansion, slavery, state's rights, and the women's movement.

Authors from this period included Washington Irving, Edgar Allen Poe, Ralph Waldo Emerson, William Cullen Bryant, James Fenimore Cooper, Margaret Fuller, Harriet Beecher Stowe, Frederic Douglas, Elizabeth Cady Stanton, Henry David Thoreau, Herman Melville, Mark Twain, and Emily Dickinson. Native American stories also began to interrupt the ethics of American democracy as Black Hawk and Tecumseh became legendary figures that represented independence and self-reliance, even among defeat.

The market for magazine and newspaper subscriptions reached record levels through the 1800s giving new forums for American writers in all types of genres and forms such as short stories, poetry, essays, politics, and travel.

Popular writers, such as Mark Twain and Washington Irving, encouraged more amateur writers to experiment in humorous, short story forms that depicted experiences of individuals in rural and frontier communities. Many of these short stories were written by businessman, preachers, attorneys, and teachers, like Rob Morris. Through his subscription business, Morris became familiar with the most popular magazines and newspapers as he traveled through Mississippi.

Morris dabbled in various literary genre that ranged from poetry, plantation novel, short stories, diaries, solicitations, instructional manuals (for masonry), travel logs, and the arrangement of lyrics for hymns. He represented the self-made individual molded by the American dream and his extensive travel through the masonic network made him a social media figure of the time. He recognized the freedom of spirit being idealized by Western expansion while giving structure to these pioneer communities through fraternal organization. He respected women and recognized their right for equal opportunity.

Rob Morris' belief in the goodness of humankind and his commitment to peaceful interventions, even during the tumultuous period of the Civil War, provided a sense of stability during a very fragmented time of American history. He can be credited for moving Freemasonry forward to the next century in a positive way, expanding charitable works from Masonic organizations that have benefitted millions throughout the world.

Picture of Rob Morris in his later years.

This organ which is now in the Rob Morris historic home, was from the Presbyterian Church in LaGrange where the Morris family attended.

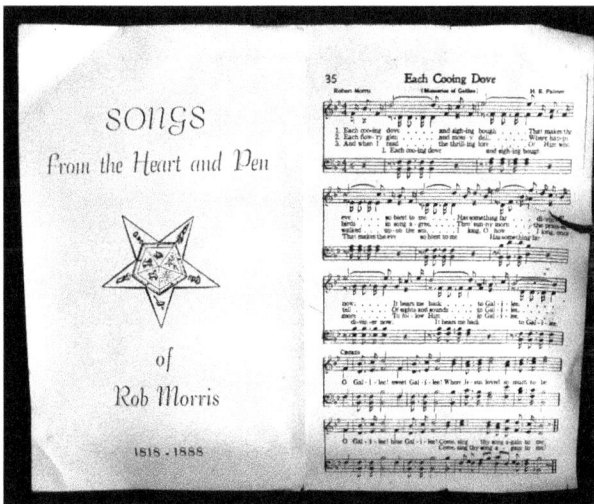

Rob Morris wrote lyrics for hymns which are still sung in many of the Masonic lodges.

This silver brick was presented to Morris by Lady Officers of Ruth, Chapter 2 OES in Montana when Rob and Charlotte travelled extensively across the United States in the 1870s and '80s.

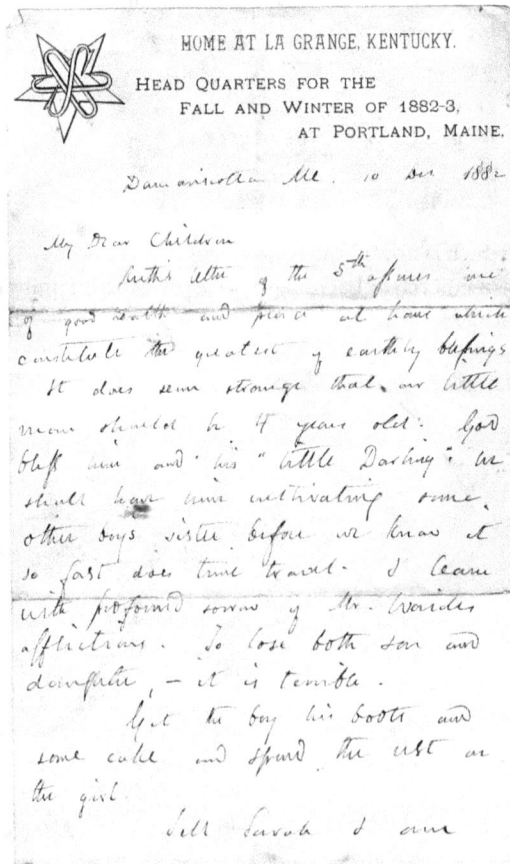

The letter heading shows Rob and Charlotte living in his home Head Quarters for the Fall and Winter 1882-83 at Portland, Maine.

Pictured in front of the Morris home is his stepson, John Mount with his wife, Ruth Morris Mount and some of their children. Rob often wrote letters to his namesake and grandson, Robbie Mount, who is pictured standing between his mother and father.

Funeral flowers and altar at the Morris home. *Courtesy of The Grand Chapter of Kentucky, OES.*

Large pinnacle gravestone marker for Rob and Charlotte
Morris at the Valley of Rest Cemetery in LaGrange.

Photograph of Charlotte Morris in later years. *Courtesy
of The Grand Chapter of Kentucky, OES.*

Charlotte Morris pictured with her grandchildren of John and Ruth Electa
Morris Mount, in front of the bedroom fireplace in the Morris home.

| MAUDE | CHARLOTTE | RUTH ELECTA | SARAH | ELLA |

Ruth Electa Morris Mount (center) is pictured with her daughters. Ella on far
right, namesake Ruth's sister who died at age 20,carried on her grandfather's legacy
and became very involved in the Order of the Eastern Star.

The Rob Morris home pictured today, is the site of an annual
pilgrimage of OES Chapters each year in August.

APPENDIX A

"Lights and Shadows of Freemasonry; consisting of Masonic Tales, Songs, and Sketches, Never Before Published" by Rob Morris, Louisville, Ky. 1852

> *I included one of Morris' humorist stories to show another side of his writing style. These collections of short stories are compositions that reflect the popularity of the humorist style of the time. They are typical of the short stories written by numerous "unknown" authors that wrote down amusing tales they had heard during their travels. Often vulgar or bawdy, they reflected the life styles of local people and their viewpoints. One of the most popular of this time was George Washington Harris (1814-1869) whose character, Sut Lovingood, inspired future writers like Mark Twain. The following is a short story from the Lights and Shadows of Freemasonry. In this composition, Morris highlights local slang and injects character traits from congregations where he was often a guest preacher. In this tale, he highlights the nobility of Masons and underscores the misconceptions perceived by the general public of this "secret" society. Morris uses italics around local vernacular to inject humor.*

The Church Trial; or, Jynin' the Masons

The Rev. Baruch Heifleberger was arraigned before the Effete congregation for jynin' the Freemasons. People cum fur and neere to see him tried. It was better nor a horse race to the folks in them diggins, and most as good as a hanging.

The members of the church, many of them, brought their families in wagons detarmed to see it out, cost what it mout.

Old Miss Slowup, the cake ooman, bright her whole stock along; so did free Josh, who makes temperance beer out of whisky and molasses; so did Sock Freelinghysen, who peddles cowbells of his own manufacture. Candidates were there, agents were there, the devil (printer's) was there. The Masons, of whom there are not many among those desolate hills mustered in full strength. Finally, there was a general turn-out, and to conclude, we were there ourself.

Parson Heidleberger's wife, who had gone sinck when she heern tell that her beloved Baruch had pitched headforemost into Masonry, got well again when she found he was likely to be expelled from the church on account of it and tuck her lord's part with infinite vivacity. She had sarched in vain for the brand; it couldn't be found.

It was the Saturday before the third Sabbath in May. Effete church was early crowded, chockful. Its seats made of rails, whose sharp edges would have aroused the sympathy of a rooster, were crowded thickly on their points of gravity, by human beings painfully balanced. The pulpit was but a pen closed on three sides, but it was crowded by five and one half preachers, come to help the breethrin try the case and degrade the criminal. The reverend monster himself was on the spot. He was an old man with thin gray hairs, tall in stature, but with a downcast look like an omphalopsychite; meek in countenance, gentle of speech, benevolent in visage-who would have thought to see him sitting there, gazing calmly around him, that he, Baruch Heidleberger, for twenty years a zealous minister, who had steemed the torrent of religious innovations, could so grievously have overstepped church rules and jyned the Masons. But he had, and here was the result. What's the world coming to? who knows?

Effete church was not al all like the temple of Luxor, either in shape or magnificence, still less did it resemble King Solomon's Temple. On the contrary it was a low dirt-daubed log cabin of a thing, a 40 by 30, plain as linsey and cold as a quaker. As Rev. Mr. Heidleberger arose in it to answer the charges ready by the moderator and to plead to the merits of the case, his bald top just reached the cross beams that bound the eends of the building together.

The charges were specific; the plead was guilty.

A hurried consultation in a hoarse whisper heard to the horse-block, and then the moderator in a confused manner begged leave to axe the the congurgashun ef he should deklar the guilty brother expended or suspelled.

Another hurried consultation-during which eleving old oomen, who wore black bonnets and no shoes, loudly clamored suspel him suspel him-after which the moderator prudently expressed the idea that had been hinted to him by one of the older members, and told Parson Heidleberger "ef he'd anything to norate in the way of vindicshun he mout."

The criminal acknowledged the courtesy by a low bow and went on in his meek, quiet way to norate:

"I feel to admit brethren beloved, (the old man differed from Webster in his orthoepy, as the reader will perceive,) I feel to admit that corin to church rules, I done wrong. Yes, I don wrong. Masontry is a securt instushun, and you all done gin in your testimonies gin securt instushuns, long ago."

A fat sort of groan from the old ladies, and a general expression of, yes, praise the Lord.

"I know that when Bob Clink got drunk and set my bakky barn to fire, you suspelled him, and when you tuck hum back, and he quit drink and huned the Sons, you suspelled him again."

An asservation, contradictory to the intention of the second commandment from the aforesaid Bob, who was present, and the chorus from the aforesaid antiquaries, yes, praise the Lord!

"But breethern, I want you to zamin this matter, tiklurly by the light of scriptur."

An interruption from the moderator who informed the bad man with great correctness, "that scriptur had nothin'to do with this matter, and eff he'd anything to norate why he juned the Masons he'd better do it to wonste."

"I ollers thought, breethern beloved," pursued the criminal with some hesitation, " I ollers thought that our church rules was the same as scriptur. Leastways that's how I ollers construed the mater for twenty, year, that I've been trying to preach the gospel and you never set me to rights afore. Well, breethern beloved, I have jyned the Masons and I'll tell you why, I did it soze to understand scripture better and bekase I thought I mout be more useful. I haint found nothing wrong in it so fur. It's a good thing. It's a blessed thing, breethern beloved. You'd all of you say 'twas good if you had it . There's mysteries in it that makes a man think better of hisself, his God and humns. There's mysteries in it. Now how many breethern and sisters is thereof you here, who'd like to know the mysteries of Masontry? Let em rise at wonste to their feet!"

Up, by a common impulse flew the crowd. Up, in spite of rheumatics and old age, the very foremost of all, flew the old women, with a Praise the Lord, half out of their throats. Up hopped the moderator, his mouth flung open gate-like from ear to ear. Up bounced Bob Clink with an oath. Up popped the Masons with surprise. Up sprung the rosy cheeked maidens with cheeks rendered yet more rosy by young men who hoped now to get out all the kernel of Masontry without havin to break the shell.

All were on the perpendicular before th echo of Parson Heidleberger's proposition had ceased to vibrate along the dusty roof.

The old gentleman glanced benevolentrly around the church, looked over the pulpit, scanned the moderator's countenance with a half smile, and went on with his exposition.

"Your curiosity, breethern beloved, is just like mine was before I jyned the Masons. Now, the Lodge ain't full yet, and if you'll do like I did, the Masons may let you in!"

The hit was too good to be overlooked. A general roar from the crowd acknowledged it. Bob Clink took a duck-fit and was carried out in spasms. The Masons clapped with their hands and stamped with their feet. The maidens giggled. The five preachers and a half (the fraction represents the moderator) and the old women, were the only serious faces.

For half an hour it seemed as if the meeting would break up without further discussion.

Silence was at length restored and old Parson Heidleberger continued his remarks, as he took a spider out of his hair that had been shaken down from the roof.

"I didn't try this plan, breethern beloved, to pick you up—not by no means. I only did it to see whether I stood alone, in curiosity to learn the secrets of Masontry. I am proud to find all the breethern and sistern in the same fix. Then I think brethren beloved, you ought to bear with me, beloved."

A tear from the old man.

"I have been in and out before you, for many a year, and it's in my heart to live and die with you."

A low shout from Mrs. Heidleberger, and weeping among the women generally, all but the aforesaid antiquated.

"I promis you, brethren, beloved, on the word of a Mason, of a Christian I mean, that my Masontry shall only make me more industrious and praying. I'll love you better, if possible, than ever I did before, beloved. And I pray the Lord to put it into your hearts to deal justly with me, breethern beloved."

But the church expelled him forthwith without a dissenting voice, and we came away.

Allen, Gloria Seaman. 1996. "Equally Their Due: Female Education in Antebellum Alexandria." *Historic Alexander Quarterly* 1 (2): 1–11.

Austin, Rev. Thomas R., LL.D. 1876. *The Well Spent Life: A Brotherly Testimonial to the Masonic Career of Robert Morris, LL.D.*, Limited Edition. Louisville, KY: Rev. Thomas Austin.

Beaderstadt, Rev. Jan L. 2003. *The Grand Luminary: A Look at the Life of Rob Morris*. Turner, MI: Coffee Times Press.

Beresniak, Daniel. 2000. *Symbols of Freemasonry*. New York, NY: Barnes and Nobles Books.

Cabaniss, Allen, P. G. M. 1976. *Freemasonry in Mississippi*. (February, 11, 1976). Meridian, MS: Grand Lodge of Mississippi.

Cato, Juanita, P. G. M. 1972. "The Order of the Eastern Star in Mississippi." *The Scottish Rite Magazine*, November, 1972.

Colton, J. H. 1855. *Mississippi Map No. 32*. New York, NY: J.H. Colton & Co.

Compton, Lisa. n.d. "The Order of the Eastern Star—Its Taunton Connection." OCHS Collection, Taunton, MA: Old Colony Historical Society.

Declaration of Sentiments. July 20, 1848. "The Elizabeth Cady Stanton and Susan B. Anthony Papers Project." Accessed 05/11/2018. http://www.ecssba.rutgers.edu/docs/ecsbday.html.

Dotson, Raymond. 1984. "Detailed Information on Rob Morris with Internet Notes of Bonita Hillmer." August 28, 1984. Lecture at Goldsboro Chapter, # 54, August 24, 1984. Accessed 05/11/2018. http://worldconnect.rootsweb.ancestry.com/cgi-bin/igm.cgi?op=GET7db jbh&idh &id=11217

Fitch, Dr. Robert. 2007. "Dr. Rob Morris, The Soldier." Unpublished transcript.

General Grand Chapter, Order of the Eastern Star. 2014. http://www.easternstar.org

Grand Secretary. 1846. *Extract of the Proceedings of the Grand Lodge of Mississippi: Grand Annual Communication*. 1846–1847. p. 67. Natchez, MI: Free Traders Office.

Hamlett, Barksdale. 1914. *History of Education in Kentucky*. Frankfort, KY: Kentucky Dept. of Education.

Harvard University Open Library. 2012. "Cholera Epidemics in the 19th Century, Contagion: Historical Views of Diseases and Epidemics." Accessed 05/11/2018 https://online-learning.harvard.edu/course/predictionx-john-snow-and-cholera-epidemic-1854?keywords=cholera

Hexon, Meg, & Staff. 2012. *Howry Family Papers 1842–1883*. University of Michigan: William L. Clements Library. Accessed 05/11/2018. https://quod.lib.umich.edu/c/clementsmss/umich-wcl-M-2328how?subview=standard;view=reslist

Hillmer, Bonita. 2014. "Morris-Peckham-Fales." Accessed 14 May 2014. accessed 05/11/2018. https://www.ancestry.com/connect/Profile/0000f621-0000-0000-0000-000000000000

Hitt, J. B, II. 2014. "J. B. Hitt Genealogy Site." Accessed 22 February 2014. http://wc.rootsweb.ancestry.com/cgi-bin/igm (currently under construction as of 05/11/2018)

Hunter, Louis. 1949. *Steamboats on the Western Rivers: An Economic and Technological History*. Cambridge, MA: Harvard Press.

Kenaston, Jean M'Kee. 1917. *History of the Order of the Eastern Star with an Authentic Biography of the Founder, Rob Morris, L.L.D*. Bonestreet, S.D.: The Torch Press.

Lazar, Zolton. 1997–2014. "Royal Solomon Mother Lodge in Israel." Lecture delivered before the John Ross Robertson Chapter of the Philalethes Society, Toronto, Canada, Reprint "The Israeli Freemason." accessed 05/11/2018 http://www.mastermason.com/fmisrael/royal.html

Lexington Royal Arch Chapter. 1848. *Royal Arch Chapter Lodge Book*. Nov. 9, 1848. Holmes County, MS: Lexington Royal Arch Chapter Nine.

Longworth's New York Register and City Directory For the Forty-Third Year of American Independence. January 1, 1818. "List of Duties, Banks, Insurance Companies & Post Office Establishment Sic., January 1, 1818." Date Accessed 05/11/2018.http://search.ebscohost.com/login.aspx?direct=true&db=h5b&AN=65275602&site=ehost-%20%20%20%20%20live&ppid=divp196

MacNulty, W. Kirk. 1991. *Freemasonry: A Journey through Ritual and*

Symbol. New York, NY:Thames & Hudson.

Maryland Historical Society. 2011. William Wirt Papers, 1784–1864. Accessed 05/11/2018 http://www.mdhs.org/findingaid/william-wirt-papers-1784-1864-ms-1011

Massachusetts, Town and Vital Records. 1620–1988. [database online]. Provo, UT: Accessed 05/11/2018 https://search.ancestry.com/search/db.aspx?dbid=2495

Moore, Charles. 1847. *Freemason's Monthly Magazine.* Vol. 6. Boston, MA: Tuttle & Dennett.

Morris, Rob. 1852. *The Faithful Slave.* Boston, MA: Ossian E. Dodge.

Morris, Rob. 1852. *The Lights and Shadows of Freemasonry, Consisting of Masonic Tales, Songs and Sketches.* Louisville, KY: J.F. Brennan, Pb.

Morris, Rob. 1859. *The History of Freemasonry in Kentucky.* Louisville, KY: Rob Morris, Pb.

Morris, Rob. 1860. *Freemason's Almanac.* Louisville, KY: Morris & Monsarrat.

Morris, Rob. 1868–1869. *The Voice of Masonry, Devoted to Masonic and General Literature, Original and Selected.* Louisville, KY: B.F. Brennan.

Morris, Rob. 1875. *Masonic Odes and Poems.* New York, NY: William T. Anderson.

Morris, Rob. 1876. *Freemasonry in the Holy Land or Handmarks of Hiram's Builders.* Chicago, IL: Knight & Leonard, Printers.

Morris, Rob. 1883. *William Morgan or Political Anti-Masonry; Its Rise, Growth and Decadence.* New York, NY: Robert MaCoy, Masonic Publisher.

Morris, Rob. 1895. *The Poetry of Freemasonry.* Chicago, IL: The Werner Company.

Morris Family Collection. 1847–1859. Unpublished Letters & Correspondence of the Morris Family. LaGrange, KY: Kentucky Chapter, Order of the Eastern Star, Courtesy of Davis Morgan & Margie Morgan Applegate.

National Register of Historic Places. 1970. "Rob Morris Little Red Schoolhouse, O.E.S. Shrine Eureka Masonic College." Entry No. 70.11.28.0014.

New England Historical and Genealogical Register. 1875. "New England

Historical and Genealogical Register." 29: 204.

Oldham County Historical Society. n.d. *Kentucky Masonic College: Funk Seminary Notebook.* LaGrange, KY: J. Chilton Barnett Archives.

Oldham County Historical Society. 1824–1864. *Slave Papers.* LaGrange, KY: J. Chilton Barnett Archives.

Oldham County Historical Society. 1884. *Rob Morris Poet Laureate Papers.* LaGrange, KY: J. Chilton Archives.

Oldham County Historical Society. 1888. *Rob Morris Funeral Procession papers and notebook.* LaGrange, KY: J. Chilton Barnett Archives.

Oldham County Historical Society. 1889. *Rev. H. R.Coleman Circular.* LaGrange, KY: J. Chilton Barnett Archives.

Patterson, K. D. 1992. "Yellow Fever Epidemics and Mortality in the U.S. 1693–1905." *Social Science Medicine.* April, 34 (8): 855–865.

Peters, Gerhard. 2014. "Election of 1832." The American Presidency Project. Accessed 05/11/2018. http//www.presidency.ucsb.edu/showelection.php?year=1832

Pond, Annie M. 1950. *Interesting Historical Data. Order of the Eastern Star, Order of the Eastern Star.* New York, NY: Order of the Eastern Star of the State of New York.

Riccards, Michael P. 1997. *The Ferocious Engine of Democracy: A History of the American Presidency, Vol. I.* New York, NY: Madison Books.

Rich, Paul. 1997. "Recovering a Rite: The Amaranth, Queen of the South, and Eastern Star." *Heredom—The Transition of the Scottish Rite Research Society,* Vol. 6. Washington, DC: The Scottish Rite Research Society. Accessed March 21 2014. http://paulrich.net/publications/heredom_02.html

Roberts, Marie. n.d. "Robert Burns, The Freemasons' Poet Laureate." Accessed 13 June 2013. http://www.lodge76.wanadoo.co.uk/the_freemason%27_poet_laureate.htm

Robertson, J. Ross. 1899. *The History of Freemasonry in Canada From Its Introduction in 1749. Vol. II.* Toronto, Canada. The Hunter Rose Co.

Rosenburg, Charles E. 1987. *The Cholera Years: The U. S. in 1832, 1849, 1866.* Chicago, IL: University of Chicago Press.

Ross, Peter. 1899. *A Standard History of Freemasonry,* New York, NY: The

Lewis Publishing Co.

Rule, Lucien. 1922. *Pioneering in Masonry: The Life and Times of Rob Morris.* Louisville, KY: Brandt & Connors Co., Inc.

Taunton Geneaology (in Bristol County). 2014. "Taunton Vital Records." Accessed 13 March 2014. accessed May 11, 2018. http://mavitalrecords.org/MA/Bristol/Taunton/Images/Taunton_M363.shtml

The Committee. 1884. *A Monument of Gratitude.* Louisville, KY: The Committee of the Order of the Eastern Star.

The Freemason Monthly. 1848. *The Freemason Monthly Magazine.* November, 1848. Boston, MA: pp. 26–27.

United States Congress. 2014. *Biographical Directory of the United States Congress: Grundy,* Accessed 05/11/2018. http://bioguide.congress.gov/scripts/biodisplay.pl?index=g000509 accessed 05/11/2018

Valso. 2014. "What Happened to Yellow Jack Part II: Antebellum Mobile and the South." Accessed 30 October 2014. http://modmobilian.com/2014/01/what-happened-to-yellow-jack-part-ii-mobile-the-south.

Voorhis, Harold Van Buren. 1958. *The Eastern Star: The Evolution from a Rite to an Order.* MaCoy Publishing and Masonic Supply Co., Inc., Richmond, VA: MaCoy Publishing and Masonic Supply Co., Inc.

Letter Collection

The primary source for this book comes from a series of over 200 unpublished letters that were collected by Marjorie Pollard Morgan Applegate and her first husband, Davis "Zeke" Morgan. These letters, handed down through family members spanned from 1848 to 1860. The letters were hand-sewn together by Charlotte Mendenhall Morris. The letters were donated by the Morgans to the Grand Chapter Kentucky, Order of the Eastern Star. The letters gave context to Morris' life and helped to clarify Rob Morris' activities and relationships. The author copied, indexed, and transcribed the letters for this manuscript.

ABOUT THE AUTHOR

Nancy Stearns Theiss, PhD., is the Executive Director of the Oldham County Historical Society. Nancy has published several books and written history columns for the Louisville Courier-Journal newspaper. She conducts oral histories of local individuals which are published as Living Treasures in the Oldham Era newspaper.

She and her husband are natives of Oldham County and live on the family farm close to LaGrange, Ky., where Morris' name is still a household word. Nancy often visited the Rob Morris' Historic home as a child which peaked her curiosity about Morris' accomplishments in freemasonry and the Order of the Eastern Star.

The Oldham County Historical Society operates a history center that includes The Peyton Samuel Family Museum, J. Chilton Barnett Archives, and Library and Rob Morris Educational Center. The educational center was the former Presbyterian Church where Dr. Rob Morris attended, lectured, and recited his poetry. The Oldham County History Center has received two designations by the National Park Service National Underground Railroad Network which are the J. C. Barnett Library and Archives (former James and Amanda Mount house) and the Henry Bibb Escapes/Gatewood Plantation archaeology site in Trimble County.

Feel free to contact Nancy at: nancystheiss@gmail.com

www.ingramcontent.com/pod-product-compliance
Lightning Source LLC
Chambersburg PA
CBHW062053270326
41931CB00013B/3052